DELIA'S
CAKES

DELIA'S
CAKES

Photography by Dan Jones
Food Stylist Lindsey Greensted Benech

HODDER &
STOUGHTON

CONTENTS

CELEBRATION CAKES

DESSERT CAKES

✳ *For gluten-free information see page 24.*

THIS BOOK IS ALL ABOUT CAKES,
but actually it's about a lot more than that. The whole affair
from start to finish is about supreme unadulterated pleasure. Or
as someone once said, when you offer homemade cake to anyone
it never fails to put a smile on their face.

But there's more. Actually setting about making a cake, allowing
your creative powers to come into play, knowing all those smiles
that await you, has a kind of hidden social agenda – it's cheaper
than therapy and much more pleasurable.

If all that sounds a bit OTT, I promise you it isn't. On the serious
side, sometimes affluence can rebound on us and in subtle ways
we can end up actually being impoverished. Cakes are a perfect
example. We now pay twice as much for mass-produced cakes
and biscuits made in factories, which will always be inferior to
and blander than homemade (not to mention the long lists of
obscure additives in the ingredients).

So if I might put a positive spin on our current climate of
austerity, what homemade cakes have got going for them is
that they provide you with something really luxurious at very
little cost. A chain coffee-house muffin circa 2013 can cost six
or seven times as much as a vastly superior homemade version.

This is where I come in, because as always I am here to try to make it as easy as possible for you to make your own cakes and biscuits for the rest of your life. And for the first time, everything will be made even more simple and accessible by the accompanying Deliaonline Cookery School (see page 25). So no excuses – you must now go and make a cake for family or friends at the first opportunity.

Happy Cake Making
Love
Delia

THE TYRANNY OF TINS

I could write a whole book just on this subject. Over the years I have constantly had to re-jig cake recipes because the required tin sizes were no longer available. And this is the predominant reason more often than not that cake recipes sometimes fail – that is, you are simply not using the correct tin for the mixture.

The tin sizes I used in my first *Book of Cakes* in 1977 were no longer sold when we published my *Baking Collection* in 2005, so we re-tested them all for different sized tins. Now, for this book in 2013, those sizes are no longer around!

It goes like this: add a few centimetres more to a tin and you can charge more. Reduce it by a few centimetres and it will be cheaper to make, so you can charge less and undercut the other guy. Translate that into what happens in the kitchen and we have the problem of eggs, which unfortunately don't come in half or quarter sizes.

Let me explain the science. Sponge cakes go like this: mixtures containing 2 eggs and 115g each of flour, sugar and butter need 18cm tins, while 3 egg and 175g mixtures need 20cm tins. Ah yes, you will think, you can easily buy such tins (although there was a time when there were no 18cm tins at all!). But think again, or rather get your tape-measure out and check them. And while you're at it they both need to be 4cm deep (because the depth of the tin encourages the cake to rise). You will find that quite a few tins stating these sizes don't actually measure up.

But now for the good news. I and the team at the Deliaonline Cookery School have collaborated with what is, in our opinion, one of the best-quality bakeware manufacturers in the country to create a range of cake tins that not only fit our recipes but will also last a lifetime. Silverwood are an established, family-run, British business and their high-quality bakeware is still partially made by hand. You can visit them if you wish, and you can see the tins being made on our website.

We have kept the entire range to a minimum, so your cupboards need no longer be clogged up with now obsolete versions circa 1970, 1980 or 1990. There are just 12 items in the range (see opposite).

Does this mean the recipes here can only be made in these tins? No, it doesn't, but you will need to find the nearest size, and remember a larger or smaller tin than the one stated will require an adjustment in cooking times (i.e. a larger tin will need less time, and a smaller tin will take more time). The Preserved Ginger Cake on page 82, for instance, from the first *Book of Cakes,* has remained extremely popular with those who follow my recipes – the original tin has not been available for years and still people have managed to make it. So, where there's a will there's a way!

In order to keep things really simple, we do not feel the need to use spring-form tins. They tend not to wear well as the clips break, and anyway removing a cake from a tin is extremely simple with a loose-based tin (see picture below). In addition, the flat loose bases of these tins are perfect for lifting cakes onto serving dishes.

HOW TO REMOVE CAKES FROM TINS

Sponge cakes are always turned out (see recipes). Other cakes can be removed by first loosening the edges by sliding a palette knife all round, then placing the cake on an upturned bowl and gently sliding the tin downwards. Then use a palette knife gently to slide the cake from the base and liner onto a cooling rack.

BAKING EQUIPMENT

CAKE TIN LINERS

Lining cake tins was always a bother and so off-putting in the old days. Not so now, because the makers of silicone or non-stick parchment papers provide packs of base liners and rolls of side lining.

However, having worked our way through the whole range of recipes in this book, we have been totally converted to cake-liners called Bake-O-Glide. They are simply a joy to use – nothing sticks every time they're used. They can be rinsed under the tap, dried with kitchen paper and used again and again, so you never run out – they're always there like a reliable friend to help make your life simpler.

We have also teamed up with the makers of Bake-O-Glide and with Silverwood, so that you can now buy the exact fit for every cake recipe in the repertoire (see picture above), including our own design for the oblong and Swiss Roll tins, plus a special baking sheet.

OTHER EQUIPMENT

SCALES

These are now electronic, light and inexpensive. It is so convenient to be able to weigh any container, press to zero and then weigh out your ingredients. (A warning, though – the batteries sometimes give up without warning, so always have plenty to spare.)

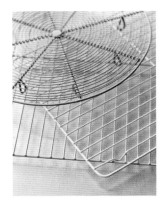

COOLING TRAYS

A quick check-list should include two wire cooling trays. Cakes will be soggy and steamy underneath if air is not allowed to circulate while they cool.

MEASURING JUGS

For liquids. It is important to check that the measurements on the side are clear to read.

PASTRY BRUSHES

These are also useful for brushing away crumbs when you want to deal with toppings and icings.

OVEN THERMOMETER

Because ovens do vary in spite of
what the temperature gauge may say.
If in doubt pop a thermometer in and
it will tell you precisely what the reading
should be. If your oven is not correct
you can call the manufacturers to get
it checked and adjusted.

MEASURING SPOONS

I have to confess I have never liked
measuring spoon sets because a)
they vary, and b) I've always thought
they were a bit mean. So I use
conventional, old-fashioned teaspoons
(5ml), dessertspoons (10ml) and
tablespoons (20ml).

ROLLING PIN

Should be wooden, long and plain,
with no grooves or handles.

MINI-CHOPPER

This is another essential in my
kitchen. Kenwood again. It chops
nuts in moments and makes light
work of purées for icings, etc.

KNIVES

Cutting cakes neatly is important, because they can get crumbly or squashed very easily. We find a sharp cook's knife (measuring 18cm) is best and to use a gentle sawing movement. A serrated knife – again with gentle sawing movements – is the one to use for cutting sponge cakes horizontally. You will also need two palette knives, one large and the other small, for spreading.

PAPER CASES

Muffin and cup cake cases are now available absolutely everywhere and come in all colours. But now you can also buy traditional tin liners – the ones with little pleats – for loaf tins and round tins, which are great for some keeping cakes (as keeping the liners on helps to prevent them drying at the edges).

SPATULAS

A proper rubber spatula will get every trace of cake mixture out of the bowl in seconds. We recommend Rubbermaid.

CUTTERS

We've used 5cm, 6.5cm and 9cm plain round cutters in this book. We have also used a gingerbread man cutter (see page 166) and an angel cutter (see page 204).

KITCHEN TIMER

Absolutely essential for all cake making and nut roasting. I have thrown out more burnt nuts than I can remember and, believe me, you simply cannot guess what time you put the cake in. Timers on mobile phones are also good.

SIEVES

For sifting flour. It's worth noting that when sieving soft fruit it's essential to have a nylon sieve.

ELECTRIC HAND WHISK

For me this is an essential piece of kitchen equipment anyway, but it really comes into its own with cakes. The best one I've ever used is the sturdy Kenwood kMix, which is very powerful and really packs a punch.

GRATERS

Box graters do everything, but it's also useful to have a nutmeg grater with a nutmeg compartment and a zester for citrus fruits.

STORING CAKES

Airtight cake tins are best for most cakes, but for delicate cakes and those destined for the refrigerator we have used a polythene cake-sized box. In this case you place the cake on the lid of the box on a flat surface and fix the rest of the container on top. The grip-lock versions are especially good for this.

For stockists of some of my favourite pieces of baking equipment, see page 224.

Freezing cakes: Most cakes can be stored in the freezer, but not for too long. We would recommend no more than a month. What is so useful about this is that if you can only use half the cake, the rest can be frozen. But perhaps the most important advantage of all in freezing is that if you live alone you can still make a beautiful cake, then wrap it in slices in freezer-proof clingfilm and place these in a polythene box and just take out a slice as and when you feel like it.

A FEW POINTERS

Is it cooked? Basically there are three ways of telling: i) if it shrinks slightly away from the side of the tin, ii) if the centre feels springy when lightly touched with the middle finger, and iii) some people like to use a skewer in the centre and if it comes out clean the cake is cooked. Not so sure about this because if you happen to stick the skewer right through a currant or a date or other sticky ingredients it can't actually come out clean. So if you're using a skewer bear this in mind. One very important point is not to panic and open the door to see how it's cooking. What this does is send cold air rushing in and spoils the cooking process. So never open the oven door till the cake has had three-quarters of its cooking time.

What if it sinks? Sometimes cakes do dip in the centre. We have pointed this out in the recipes where it's applicable. But the best thing to do is to ignore it, and remember a homemade cake is full of beautiful ingredients and, whatever its appearance, it will always taste good.

What about failures? There really shouldn't be any if – and it's a big if – you follow the recipe exactly, use the right sized tin, make sure the temperature is correct and keep a sharp eye on the timing. But just to give you a bit more reassurance, if a recipe doesn't work there's usually something wrong with the recipe rather than the way it's followed. So I'll leave you with this thought: if you have a failure, it's my fault!

USING THE RIGHT INGREDIENTS

Thankfully, the majority of cake ingredients are simple, everyday items that need little explanation. We have throughout this book opted for simplicity and the 'less is more' rule, as too many ingredients clogging up cupboards are more hassle (and there's less to throw out when it doesn't get used).

BUTTER

We think we now have the final word on this. The old-fashioned method of cake-making (i.e. first cream the butter and sugar, then add the eggs. Don't let it curdle or it lets the air escape) has almost gone – we have only one cake in this book that needs it.

When the first edition was published the arrival of soft whipped vegetable fat was in a way liberating, because you could make a cake by whipping up all the ingredients together (an all-in-one) and this may still suit some vegetarians best. It does make a very, very light cake indeed. There was only one problem: the loss of the wonderful flavour of butter. So we moved on and started to make cakes with very soft butter.

This was fine, except that getting block butter soft was always a real pain and you could never be spontaneous.

Now at last the problem is well and truly solved, as we can buy what's called spreadable butter that can be used straight from the fridge. What's happened is that some oil has been added to make it spreadable and, in our case, perfect for instant cake-making.

What we've also discovered is that a little oil in the butter is good for the cake and keeping it moist. These so-called spreadable butters do, however, vary and we have found Lurpak is the best because it has the highest butter content, and because it has the least additives it is the purest.

BLOCK BUTTER

We still use this throughout the book whenever a recipe calls for melted butter.

EGGS
Again, to make things easier, we have used all large sized free-range eggs.

FLOUR
In this case simplicity has been achieved by just using plain and self-raising with baking powder and sometimes bicarbonate of soda.

VANILLA EXTRACT
We like Fairtrade Ndali the best, and we've come to the conclusion there's no need for you to be stripping out seeds from pods or using paste. Pure, simple extract is all you need.

PURE ALMOND EXTRACT
Just to say, make sure the word 'extract' is on the bottle, and not 'essence'.

CHOCOLATE
We have used Green and Black's Fairtrade chocolate throughout, 70% cocoa solid for dark chocolate, 37% for milk chocolate – as well as their Fairtrade cocoa powder.

OTHER INGREDIENTS

SPECIALIST FRUITS

We have discovered a supplier who will provide everything you need with superb quality, for example pinhead currants, which are smaller and contain fewer seeds, Lexia raisins which are made from dried Muscat grapes, whole candied peels and many others (see page 224).

SPICES

There are important things to say about spices – not just in cakes but in all cooking, namely how to conserve their flavour, particularly once they are ground. There are two enemies of flavour. The first is light, the second is air. Spices sold in glass jars are displayed under constantly glaring lights. Then once the jar is opened, as more and more is used, it is exposed to more and more air. For this reason I now only buy spices from a firm called Seasoned Pioneers. The spices are high quality, and they cleverly pack them in foil packs to shield them from the light. Then when you begin to use them you can reseal them, eliminating any air. They have a very good online or postal service (see page 224).

SPECIAL INGREDIENTS

Wherever these apply throughout the book, we will within the recipe direct you to a suppliers list on page 224.

FAIRTRADE

There is something communal about making a cake, and to know that buying ingredients from small suppliers around the world whose livelihoods depend on it is very satisfying. I am a huge supporter of the Fairtrade movement and, wherever possible, we have used their ingredients (dried fruits, sugars, vanilla extract and so on) which also happen to be superb quality.

GLUTEN-FREE
CAKES & BISCUITS

We are very happy to report that we have tested all the recipes in this book with gluten-free ingredients. And we're even happier to tell all gluten-free cake-makers that we have been most impressed with the results. Sometimes the cakes might be a little more crumbly, but most of the time there is very little difference, particularly with muffins, fruit cakes and biscuits.

A small number of our recipes were not really suitable; these have been marked with an asterisk on the Contents page. ✳

The gluten-free ingredients we used are:

White flour, plain and self-raising
Baking powder
Cornflour
Cereals
Porridge oats (ground in a mini-chopper to replace oatmeal)
Polenta

The following cakes contain no gluten:

Squidgy Chocolate Cake
Moist Chocolate & Rum Squares
Chocolate Soufflé Cake *with* Armagnac Prunes & Crème Fraiche Sauce
Apricot Hazelnut Meringue Cake

EGG-FREE CAKES & BISCUITS

Marmalade Cake
Flapjacks
Apricot Oat Slices
Chocolate Marbled Energy Bars
Sticky Prune & Date Cake
Viennese Tartlets
Gingerbread Men
Spiced Date & Sesame Crunchies
Semolina Shortbreads

Whole Oat Crunchies
Grasmere Ginger Shortbread
Crystallised Ginger Oat Biscuits
Gingernuts
Chocolate Orange Biscuits
Florentines
Garibaldi Biscuits, Eccles Cakes (omit the egg white glaze and simply sprinkle with the sugar before baking)

THE DELIAONLINE
COOKERY SCHOOL

In the past there have been many books published in conjunction with TV series, but this is the first time a book has been published to coincide with the launch of an online cookery school, of which the first term will be dedicated to cakes.

I am aware that a quarter of the population does not own a computer and that there is still a big demand for cookery books, but to own a book and alongside that be able to see certain basic skills and cooking techniques demonstrated in your own home – or anywhere at all – at any time seems to me to be the very best of all worlds. So I hope at some stage you'll be able to enjoy both. The other wonderful advantage of the internet is that now I can answer directly any questions you may have about the recipes, or cake-making in general, on one of our regular live webchats.

www.deliaonline.com

Sponge Cakes

CLASSIC SPONGE CAKE

This is where it all begins: what I am aiming to do here is get you started on
cake making. Once you have mastered the art of the classic sponge cake you can then
move on to all the variations and never look back. The best bit is that from now on you are
going to know just how easy it is.

115g self-raising flour ◆ 1 level teaspoon baking powder ◆ 115g spreadable butter
115g golden caster sugar ◆ 2 large eggs ◆ 1 teaspoon vanilla extract

To finish: preserves, etc (see below) ◆ icing sugar

Two 18cm by 4cm sponge tins, lightly buttered and bases lined (see page 13),
plus two wire cooling trays
Pre-heat the oven to 170ºC, gas mark 3

All you do is sift the flour and baking powder into a roomy mixing bowl,
lifting the sieve quite high to give the flour a good airing as it goes down, then simply
add all the other ingredients. Now, using an electric hand whisk, combine them for
about 1 minute until you have a smooth creamy consistency.

Next divide the mixture between the two prepared tins, level off using the back of
a tablespoon, and bake near the centre of the oven for about 25 minutes. The cakes are
cooked when you press lightly with your little finger and the centre springs back.

Remove them from the oven and after about 30 seconds loosen the edges by sliding
a palette knife all round then turn them out onto a wire cooling tray. Now carefully peel
back the lining by gently pulling it back. Lightly place the other cooling tray on top and
just flip them both over so that the tops are facing upwards (this is to prevent them
sticking to the cooling tray).

When cool, sandwich them together with any sort of preserve or lemon curd, with or
without fresh whipped cream (in the summer fresh berries and cream make a superb filling).
For a final flourish, dust the whole cake generously with icing sugar.

Store in a tin or, if you are using cream, in a polythene box in the fridge.

SWISS ROLL

Will anyone still make a Swiss roll? we asked ourselves. We made one and guess what, it was absolutely lovely, so here it is, and actually it's very easy to make.

110g self-raising flour ◆ 1 level teaspoon baking powder ◆ 50g spreadable butter ◆ 2 large eggs
110g golden caster sugar, plus a little extra ◆ 1 teaspoon vanilla extract

For the filling and topping: 3–4 tablespoons jam ◆ caster sugar to finish

A Silverwood Swiss Roll tin 20cm by 30cm, greased and lined with a single sheet of baking
parchment or liner (see page 13), so that it comes up 2.5cm above the edge of the rim
Pre-heat the oven to 200°C, gas mark 6

First sift the flour and baking powder into a roomy mixing bowl, lifting the sieve quite high to give the flour a good airing as it goes down. Then add the butter, eggs, caster sugar and vanilla extract, and using an electric whisk mix to a smooth creamy consistency for about one minute.

Next, spread the mixture evenly in the prepared tin with the back of a tablespoon and don't worry if it looks a bit sparse because it will 'puff up' quite a lot. Bake it near the centre of the oven for 14–15 minutes or until it feels springy in the centre.

While it's cooking you can prepare everything for the rolling operation. First of all you need a damp tea towel spread out on a flat surface (and a second one ready for later), then on top of the tea towel you place a sheet of baking parchment that's about 2.5cm larger than the tin. Then sprinkle caster sugar all over the paper.

As soon as the Swiss roll is cooked, lift it out holding the sides of the liner and turn it onto the paper immediately. Now carefully and gently strip off the liner, take a sharp knife and trim 3mm from all round the cake. This will make it much neater and help to prevent it from cracking.

Cover with a clean damp tea towel and leave for a couple of minutes, then remove the damp cloth and spread the cake with jam. Then with one of the shorter edges of the cake nearest to you, make a small incision about 2.5cm from the edge, cutting right across the cake, not too deeply; this will help you when you start to roll. Now start to roll this 2.5cm piece over and away from you and continue to roll, holding the sugared paper behind the cake as you roll the whole thing up. When it's completely rolled up, hold the paper around the cake for a few moments to help it 'set' in position, then transfer the cake to a wire cooling tray. Dust with a little more caster sugar before serving.

If you've never made a Swiss roll before, I can assure you this *sounds* much more complicated than it actually is. The whole operation should only take a few minutes.

COFFEE & WALNUT SPONGE CAKE

This is a revised, more contemporary, version of one of the original sponge cakes in the earlier book. I am still very fond of it and have continued to make it regularly over the years. Now, though, since the advent of mascarpone, the icing is a great improvement.

115g self-raising flour ◆ 1 level teaspoon baking powder ◆ 115g spreadable butter
2 large eggs ◆ 115g golden caster sugar ◆ 1 rounded tablespoon instant espresso coffee powder
50g walnuts, very finely chopped

For the filling and topping: 250g mascarpone ◆ 1 rounded dessertspoon instant espresso coffee powder
1 tablespoon golden caster sugar ◆ 1–2 tablespoons milk ◆ 8 walnut halves

Two 18cm by 4cm sponge tins, lightly buttered and bases lined (see page 13),
plus two wire cooling trays
Pre-heat the oven to 170ºC, gas mark 3

Start off by sifting the flour and baking powder into a roomy mixing bowl, holding the sieve quite high to give the flour a good airing as it goes down, then add the butter, eggs, caster sugar and coffee powder. Now, using an electric hand whisk, mix to a smooth, creamy consistency for about 1 minute. After that take a tablespoon and fold the chopped nuts into the mixture.

Next divide the mixture between the two prepared tins, level off using the back of a tablespoon and bake near the centre of the oven for about 25 minutes. The sponges are cooked when you press lightly with your little finger and the centre springs back. Remove them from the oven and after about 30 seconds loosen the edges by sliding a palette knife all round then turn them out onto a wire cooling tray. Now carefully peel back the lining by gently pulling it back. Then lightly place the other cooling tray on top and just flip them both over so that the tops are facing upwards (this is to prevent them sticking to the cooling tray).

While the cakes are cooling, make up the filling: in a small bowl combine the mascarpone, coffee powder and caster sugar with 1 tablespoon of milk – what you need is a smooth spreadable consistency. As some mascarpones are wetter than others it's impossible to be precise, but add a bit more milk if you think it needs it.

When the cakes are cold, spread half the filling over one, sandwich them together, then spread the rest over the top using a palette knife and making a swirling pattern. Then finish off by placing the walnuts in a circle near the edge. Store in a polythene box in the fridge.

ICED LEMON CURD LAYER CAKE

This one's always been a winner with my family and friends – it's even become a much-requested birthday cake. This time round we've added a whipped cream and lemon curd icing to make it even more special. Although the mixture is a 3 egg, 175g mix we are using the same size tins as for the other sponges, which means you will have a much deeper cake because we need four layers.

175g self-raising flour ◆ 1 level teaspoon baking powder ◆ 175g spreadable butter
175g golden caster sugar ◆ 3 large eggs ◆ grated zest of 1 large lemon ◆ 1 tablespoon lemon juice

For the lemon curd: zest and juice of 1½ large lemons ◆ 110g golden caster sugar
3 large eggs ◆ 75g block butter

For the icing: 150ml double cream ◆ 1 lemon, zested (on top)

Two 18cm by 4cm sponge tins, lightly buttered and bases lined (see page 13),
plus two wire cooling trays
Pre-heat the oven to 170ºC, gas mark 3

All you do is sift the flour and baking powder into a roomy mixing bowl, lifting the sieve quite high to give the flour a good airing as it goes down, then simply add all the other ingredients and, using an electric hand whisk, combine them for about 1 minute until you have a smooth creamy consistency.

Next divide the mixture between the two prepared tins, level off using the back of a tablespoon and bake on the centre shelf of the oven for about 25 minutes. The cakes are cooked when you press lightly with your little finger and the centre springs back.

Remove them from the oven and after about 30 seconds loosen the edges by sliding a palette knife all round then turn them out onto a wire cooling tray. Now carefully peel back the lining by gently pulling it back. Lightly place the other cooling tray on top and just flip them both over so that the tops are facing upwards (this is to prevent them sticking to the cooling tray).

While the cakes are cooking you can make the lemon curd: place the grated lemon zest and sugar in a bowl, whisk the lemon juice together with the eggs, and pour this over the sugar. Next add the butter cut into small pieces, and place the bowl over a pan of barely simmering water (making sure the bowl does not touch the water). Whisk every now and then until thickened, which should take about 20 minutes. Then leave it on one side to cool.

When the cakes are absolutely cold – and not before – carefully cut each one horizontally into two with a good sharp serrated knife. I have always found the best way to do this is to sit down with the sponge cakes on a board, hold each one steady with one hand and then, using a gentle sawing movement, slice through each one so you end up with four layers.

Now use the lemon curd to sandwich the cakes together, reserving 2 slightly rounded tablespoons (for the icing). Then whisk the cream till thickened, fold the remaining lemon curd into the cream and use it to ice the cake by spreading it over the top first then carefully down the sides, using a palette knife. Sprinkle with the lemon zest before serving. Store in a polythene box in the fridge till needed.

MAPLE & CARAMELISED PECAN CAKE

I have been a huge fan of maple syrup ever since I went to Canada to see how it was produced. It has a unique flavour, which seems to have a real affinity with pecan nuts. And using the syrup to caramelise them gives a lovely crunchy texture.

115g self-raising flour ◆ 1 level teaspoon baking powder ◆ 115g spreadable butter ◆ 2 large eggs
115g golden caster sugar ◆ 1 tablespoon pure maple syrup (Amber No. 2 if possible)
50g pecan nuts, very finely chopped

For the filling and topping: 100g pecan nuts, roughly chopped
6 tablespoons maple syrup ◆ 250g mascarpone

Two 18cm by 4cm sponge tins, lightly buttered and bases lined (see page 13),
plus two wire cooling trays
Pre-heat the oven to 170ºC, gas mark 3

Begin by sifting the flour and baking powder into a roomy mixing bowl, lifting the sieve quite high to give the flour a good airing as it goes down, then add the butter, eggs, caster sugar and maple syrup. Now, using an electric hand whisk, mix to a smooth, creamy consistency for about one minute. After that fold the chopped nuts into the mixture with a tablespoon.

Divide the mixture between the two prepared tins, level off using the back of a tablespoon and bake near the centre of the oven for about 25 minutes. The cakes are cooked when you press lightly with your little finger and the centre springs back.

Remove them from the oven (increasing the heat to 200°C, gas mark 6) and after about 30 seconds loosen the edges by sliding a palette knife all round then turn them out onto a wire cooling tray. Now carefully peel back the lining by gently pulling it back. Lightly place the other cooling tray on top and just flip them both over so that the tops are facing upwards (this is to prevent them sticking to the cooling tray).

Next caramelise the nuts by tossing them in a bowl with 2 tablespoons of the maple syrup, then spread them out onto a small baking tray with a liner and pop them in the oven to caramelise, which will take 10 minutes – put a timer on here because if you forget them they burn very quickly!

Meanwhile combine the rest of the maple syrup with the mascarpone and then, when the nuts have cooled, spread half of this over one of the cakes, using a palette knife, and sprinkle half the cooled nuts over. Place the other cake on top and spread the rest of the mascarpone mixture over, and finally sprinkle with the rest of the nuts. Store in a polythene box in the fridge until needed.

FRESH LIME & COCONUT CAKE

This is a new adaptation of the cake in *Summer Collection*. I have to say the coconut milk powder *is* an essential ingredient, as we have tried other products which simply don't work. It's not that easy to get hold of but it's worth ordering some (see page 224) just to make this wonderful cake.

2 small limes ◆ 50g desiccated coconut ◆ 115g self-raising flour ◆ 1 level teaspoon baking powder
115g golden caster sugar ◆ 115g spreadable butter ◆ 2 large eggs
1½ tablespoons dried coconut milk powder

For the filling and topping: *zest and juice of 1 small lime ◆ 150–175g fondant icing sugar, sifted*
3 tablespoons dried coconut milk powder ◆ 1 extra lime (see recipe)

Two 18cm by 4cm sponge tins, lightly buttered and bases lined (see page 13),
plus two wire cooling trays

Begin by removing the zest of two limes either with a zester or a grater onto a piece of clingfilm, then wrap the zest in the clingfilm and leave on one side. You now need to measure the desiccated coconut into a small bowl and add the juice of both limes. Give it a stir, and leave it to soak for at least an hour.

When you are ready to make the cake, pre-heat the oven to 170°C, gas mark 3. Then sift the flour and baking powder into a roomy mixing bowl, lifting the sieve quite high to give the flour a good airing as it goes down. Then add the caster sugar, butter, eggs and coconut milk powder and whisk, with an electric hand whisk, for about 1 minute to combine them until you have a smooth creamy consistency. Then fold in the soaked coconut and the prepared lime zest.

Next divide the mixture between the two prepared tins, level off using the back of a tablespoon and bake near the centre of the oven for about 25 minutes. The cakes are cooked when you press lightly with your little finger and the centre springs back. Remove them from the oven and after about 30 seconds loosen the edges by sliding a palette knife all round then turn them out onto a wire cooling tray. Now carefully peel back the lining by gently pulling it back. Lightly place the other cooling tray on top and just flip them over so that the tops are facing upwards (this is to prevent them sticking to the cooling tray).

For the icing, take the zest from one lime (using a zester if possible), and squeeze out the juice. Put the juice and zest in a bowl, then add 150g of the sifted icing sugar a little at a time, with a wooden spoon. After that add the coconut milk powder.

Now zest the other lime, then pare off the pith (using your sharpest knife). Next take out the lime segments one at a time, slicing between the membranes. Do this over a saucer to catch the juice, allowing the segments to drop onto the saucer. If they are large, cut each one in half and add them and the juice to the icing and fold them in with a tablespoon.

The juiciness of limes can vary, so if it seems a little runny add some or all of the remaining 25g of sifted icing sugar. Then use half of the icing to sandwich the cakes together and spread the other half on top. Finally sprinkle the surface with the lime zest. Store the cake in a tin until needed.

ICED ENGLISH WALNUT CAKE

You can obviously make this with ready-shelled walnuts, but in the late autumn when English walnuts are about, if you sit down with music or a good radio programme and shell some new season's walnuts yourself, you will appreciate the purest flavour of walnuts that permeates this cake.

175g self-raising flour ◆ 1½ level teaspoons baking powder ◆ 175g spreadable butter
3 large eggs ◆ 175g golden caster sugar ◆ 75g shelled walnuts, very finely chopped

For the filling and icing: 2 large egg whites, lightly beaten ◆ a few drops vanilla extract
500g fondant icing sugar, sifted (plus extra if needed) ◆ 50g walnuts, chopped small
8–10 walnut halves (to decorate)

Two 18cm by 4cm sponge tins, lightly buttered and bases lined (see page 13), plus two wire cooling trays
Pre-heat the oven to 170°C, gas mark 3

First sift the flour and baking powder into a roomy mixing bowl, lifting the sieve quite high to give the flour a good airing as it goes down. Then add the butter, eggs and caster sugar and, using an electric whisk, mix to a smooth creamy consistency for about one minute. Next lightly fold in the finely chopped walnuts.

Then divide the mixture between the two prepared tins, level off using the back of a tablespoon, and bake near the centre of the oven for about 30 minutes. The cakes are cooked when you press lightly with your little finger and the centre springs back.

Remove them from the oven and after about 30 seconds loosen the edges by sliding a palette knife all round then turn them out onto a wire cooling tray. Now carefully peel back the lining by gently pulling it back. Lightly place the other cooling tray on top and just flip them both over so that the tops are facing upwards (this is to prevent them sticking to the cooling tray).

To make the icing, place the egg whites and vanilla in a large mixing bowl, and gradually add the icing sugar (a heaped tablespoon at a time), beating well after each addition with a wooden spoon until the icing is a smooth, soft, spreadable consistency (it should be just firm enough to stay in place). What you can do to check the consistency is to spread a little on the inside of the bowl to see if it's OK. Don't worry if you have some icing sugar left over (if your whites are very large, you may need a bit more icing sugar).

Now, when the sponges are absolutely cold, carefully cut each one into two horizontally using a sharp serrated knife. I find it's better to sit down to do this, so you don't have to bend so much to see what you are doing!

After that, keep the nicest-looking cake for the top, and spread each of the other layers with a rounded tablespoon of the icing. Then sprinkle each layer with one third of the chopped walnuts. Now sandwich the cakes together and place them on a cooling rack. Use a pastry brush to brush away

any loose crumbs, then place the rack over a large plate. Now spoon three quarters of the icing on top of the cake, and use a palette knife to spread the icing over the top and down the sides of the cake.

Use the remaining icing to patch up any exposed bits of cake. Finally wipe the palette knife and dip it into a jug of warm water, and use it to go over the icing to give a smooth neat finish. After that, decorate with the walnut halves in a circle over the top. Store the cake in a cake box or tin till needed.

COFFEE & CARDAMOM CAKE
with PISTACHIOS

A friend of a friend of mine always grinds cardamom seeds and adds them when she
drinks coffee. It has to be said the two flavours together are sublime. So here they are combined in
a very luscious cake topped with roasted pistachios.

50g shelled unsalted pistachios ◆ the seeds from 10 green cardamom pods ◆ 115g self-raising flour
1 level teaspoon baking powder ◆ 115g spreadable butter ◆ 2 large eggs ◆ 115g golden caster sugar
1 tablespoon instant espresso coffee powder

For the syrup: 1 slightly rounded dessertspoon instant espresso coffee powder
the seeds from 10 green cardamom pods
1 level tablespoon demerara sugar ◆ 25ml boiling water

For the filling and topping: 250g mascarpone ◆ 1 rounded dessertspoon instant espresso coffee powder
1 tablespoon golden caster sugar ◆ 1–2 tablespoons milk ◆ 50g shelled unsalted pistachios

Two 18cm by 4cm sponge tins, lightly buttered and bases lined (see page 13). Also a pestle and mortar
Pre-heat the oven to 170°C, gas mark 3

First of all, when the oven is pre-heated you need to roast all the pistachios (for the cake and the
topping) – just spread them out on a tray and pop them into the oven near the centre for 8 minutes –
use a timer to help you remember. While that's happening, place the 10 cardamom pods for the cake in a
mortar, bash them about to split the pods open, then remove the seeds to a saucer. Now do the same
with the 10 pods for the syrup, using a separate saucer. Next discard all the pods and grind each
lot of seeds, keeping them separate, to a fine powder. When the nuts are ready, chop half of
them finely and keep the rest on one side for the topping.

Now to make the cake. First of all, sift the flour and baking powder into a roomy mixing
bowl, lifting the sieve quite high to give the flour a good airing as it goes down. Then add the
butter, eggs, caster sugar, instant espresso and one saucer of cardamom powder, and using an electric
hand whisk, mix to a smooth, creamy consistency for about 1 minute. After that fold the chopped
nuts into the mixture with a tablespoon. Now divide the mixture between the two prepared tins,
level off using the back of a tablespoon and bake near the centre of the oven for about
25 minutes. Meanwhile you can make up the syrup and the topping.

Place the coffee powder, the other saucer of crushed cardamom and sugar in a heatproof
bowl, then measure the boiling water into it and whisk for about one minute until the coffee and sugar
have dissolved. For the filling and topping, whisk all the ingredients except the pistachios together
in another bowl.

The cakes are cooked when you press lightly with your little finger and the centre springs back.

Remove them from the oven but leave them in their tins. Prick them all over with a skewer while they are still hot and sprinkle the syrup as evenly as possible over each one, leaving them to soak up the liquid as they cool in their tins.

When they are absolutely cold, loosen the edges with a palette knife, then place each one on an upturned bowl (see page 12) and carefully slide the outer edge of the tin downwards. Choose a serving plate and, using a palette knife, gently slide one cake off its liner onto the plate. Then spread half the filling mixture over the first cake. Then (as above) slide the other cake carefully on top, and spread with the other half of the mixture. To finish, scatter the roasted pistachios all over just before serving. Store in a polythene box in the fridge until needed.

FRESH ORANGE &
PASSION FRUIT CAKE

The combination of orange and passion fruit gives this a tangy flavour, and because passion fruit is always available it's great to use between seasons, particularly in winter.

115g self-raising flour ◆ 1 level teaspoon baking powder ◆ 115g spreadable butter ◆ 2 large eggs
115g golden caster sugar ◆ zest of 1 large orange ◆ 1 tablespoon orange juice

For the filling: 2 ripe passion fruits ◆ 250g mascarpone ◆ 1 tablespoon golden caster sugar
1 teaspoon vanilla extract ◆ 3 tablespoons orange juice ◆ a little icing sugar, sifted (to finish)

Two 18cm by 4cm sponge tins, lightly buttered and bases lined (see page 13),
plus two wire cooling trays
Pre-heat the oven to 170ºC, gas mark 3

First sift the flour and baking powder into a roomy mixing bowl, lifting the sieve quite high to give the flour a good airing as it goes down. Then add the butter, eggs and caster sugar and, using an electric hand whisk, mix to a smooth, creamy consistency for about one minute. After that, using a tablespoon, fold the orange zest and 1 tablespoon of orange juice into the mixture.

Divide the mixture between the two prepared tins, level off using the back of a tablespoon and bake near the centre of the oven for about 25 minutes. The cakes are cooked when you press lightly with your little finger and the centre springs back. Remove them from the oven and after about 30 seconds loosen the edges by sliding a palette knife all round then turn them out onto a wire cooling tray. Now carefully peel back the lining by first making a fold and gently pulling it back. Lightly place the other cooling tray on top and just flip them both over so that the tops are facing upwards (this is to prevent them sticking to the cooling tray).

To make the filling, slice the passion fruits into halves, then take a small bowl and a teaspoon and scoop out all the flesh and seeds into it. In another (larger) bowl combine the mascarpone, sugar, vanilla extract and 3 tablespoons of orange juice. Then add two thirds of the passion fruit juice and seeds, and stir them in as evenly as possible.

Spread this mixture over one of the sponges, then make some indentations with a teaspoon all over and spoon the rest of the passion fruit into them. Then place the other cake on top, press it gently so the filling oozes out a little at the edges and dust the surface of the cake with sifted icing sugar just before serving. Store in a polythene box in the fridge.

STRAWBERRIES & CREAM
SPONGE CAKE

This may look a little complicated, but in fact the final result makes it so much easier to serve for a party.

115g self-raising flour ◆ ½ level teaspoon baking powder ◆ 2 large eggs
115g spreadable butter ◆ 115g golden caster sugar ◆ ½ teaspoon pure vanilla extract

For the filling and topping: 200ml double cream
350g strawberries, hulled (apart from two of them) ◆ 1 dessertspoon caster sugar
a little icing sugar (to finish)

20cm by 4cm round sponge tin, lightly greased and base lined (see page 13), plus a cooling rack
Pre-heat the oven to 170°C, gas mark 3

Begin by sifting the flour and baking powder into a large roomy bowl, lifting the sieve high to give the flour an airing. Now just add all the other ingredients and, using an electric hand whisk, whisk for about one minute until you have a smooth creamy mixture that drops off a spoon easily.

Next, spoon the mixture into the tin, levelling it with the back of the spoon, and bake near the centre of the oven for 30–35 minutes or until the centre feels springy. Leave the cake in the tin for 5 minutes before loosening the edge with a palette knife and turning it out onto a cooling rack. Now peel off the liner, turn the cake upright and let it get quite cold.

To serve the cake, first whisk the cream in a large bowl until stiff. Next you need to place the cake on a flat surface and using a serrated knife carefully split it horizontally into two thin halves. Now, leaving the two halves stacked one on top of the other, divide the cake into quarters, then each quarter into two (so you have 8 wedges of sponge cake).

Remove the top layer of wedges and arrange the bottom layer on a serving dish, re-forming it into a round. Weigh out 200g of the hulled strawberries, and whizz them to a purée with one dessertspoon of caster sugar. Now, spread half the cream over the cake and top with the remaining hulled strawberries (slicing any large ones in half and making sure the berries round the edges are showing). Spoon over the purée and cover with the other half of the cream, then re-form the top layer, making sure it lines up with the base. Dust the whole thing with icing sugar, then cut the reserved strawberries in quarters through the stalk and use to decorate the top of the cake.

Loaf Cakes

VERY FRUITY IRISH TEA CAKE

There are many versions of this and the type of tea used varies from what I call common tea to… you name it. But more importantly we have crammed in as much fruit as we could. Thus it keeps very moist and, later on, toasts beautifully.

*For the pre-soaking: 110g raisins ◆ 110g currants
110g sultanas ◆ 50g chopped candied peel ◆ 50g demerara sugar
150ml hot tea, any kind (Lapsang, Earl Grey or any other)*

*For the cake: 50g pecan nuts ◆ 1 large egg
225g self-raising flour ◆ 1–2 tablespoons milk*

*A Silverwood loaf tin (or a standard 2lb loaf tin),
lined with a 2lb traditional loaf tin liner (see page 16)*

I always find it's best to start this the night before. All you do is place the fruits and peel in a bowl, then dissolve the sugar in the hot tea and pour this over the fruits. Then cover with a cloth and leave them to soak – as the fruits absorb the tea they become plump and juicy.

When you are ready to make the cake, pre-heat the oven to 170°C, gas mark 3, then place the nuts on a baking sheet and pop them into the oven. Give them about 8 minutes to toast, but put a timer on because they burn very easily.

After they have cooled, roughly chop the nuts. Now whisk the egg and add it to the fruits and after that sift in the flour, add the toasted nuts and give everything a thorough mixing. Then add a tablespoon of milk, and if the mixture still feels stiff, stir in another. Spoon the mixture into the prepared tin, levelling off with the back of a tablespoon dipped in cold water. Then place it on a lower shelf so that the top of the tin is aligned with the centre of the oven, and bake for 1 hour 10 minutes until it feels springy in the centre.

When it comes out of the oven, turn it out onto a wire rack to cool. Serve it cut in thick slices spread generously with butter and although it does keep well in an airtight tin in its liner, it's also extremely good toasted.

BANANA & WALNUT LOAF

If I had a pound for every… goes the old cliché. So here it goes again. If only I had a pound for everyone who has praised this cake, rich pickings! Although this is made here with butter and lard, you could make it with just spreadable butter.

225g plain flour ◆ 2 level teaspoons baking powder ◆ 40g butter, at room temperature
40g lard, at room temperature
1 large egg, beaten ◆ 110g caster sugar ◆ 4 medium bananas, peeled
50g walnuts, roughly chopped ◆ zest of 1 orange and 1 lemon
1 rounded tablespoon demerara sugar

A Silverwood loaf tin (or a standard 2lb loaf tin),
lined with a 2lb traditional loaf tin liner (see page 16)
Pre-heat the oven to 180°C, gas mark 4

First sift the flour and baking powder into a roomy mixing bowl, lifting the sieve quite high to give the flour a good airing as it goes down, then add the butter, lard, egg and caster sugar. Now, using an electric hand whisk, mix to combine all the ingredients for about one minute until you have a sandy texture.

Then in a separate bowl mash the bananas to a pulp with a large fork and briefly whisk them into the cake mixture. Now fold in the chopped walnuts and orange and lemon zests. Spoon the cake mixture into the prepared tin, level it off on top with the back of the spoon and sprinkle with the demerara sugar. Bake on a lower shelf so the top of the tin is aligned with the centre of the oven for approximately 1 hour 10 minutes. Leave the cake in the tin for 10 minutes, then turn it out onto a wire cooling rack. Store in an airtight tin in its liner.

MARMALADE CAKE

I have fond memories of my friend, Molly Owen, who gave me this recipe. On paper it may sound a bit unlikely, but just you wait.

225g plain flour ◆ 3 level teaspoons baking powder ◆ 110g dark brown soft sugar
110g spreadable butter ◆ zest of 1 small orange and 1 small lemon ◆ 1 level teaspoon mixed spice
110g mixed dried fruit ◆ 150ml milk ◆ 1 teaspoon malt vinegar
1 heaped tablespoon chunky homemade Seville orange marmalade

For the topping: 1 tablespoon demerara sugar

A Silverwood loaf tin (or a standard 2lb loaf tin),
lined with a 2lb traditional loaf tin liner (see page 16)
Pre-heat the oven to 180°C, gas mark 4

First, in a large mixing bowl combine the flour, baking powder and sugar, then rub the butter into the dry ingredients until the mixture is coarsely crumbled. Add the grated lemon and orange rinds, the mixed spice and dried fruit.

Stir all these together and add the milk a little at a time, followed by the vinegar. Stir until all the ingredients are evenly distributed, then stir in the marmalade – and you should have a good dropping consistency (so that if you tap a spoonful of the mixture on the side of the bowl, it drops off easily – you can adjust this with a touch more milk if necessary).

Now spread the mixture evenly in the prepared tin using the back of a tablespoon, and sprinkle the top with the demerara sugar. Bake on a lower shelf so the top of the tin is aligned with the centre of the oven for 1¼ hours or until the cake feels firm in the centre. (After the cake has had 50 minutes, cover loosely with a piece of foil to prevent the sugar burning.) Leave to cool in the tin for 10 minutes before turning out onto a wire cooling rack. Store in its liner in an airtight tin – it does improve with keeping.

DARK JAMAICAN GINGERBREAD

This cake, originally from the sugar-and-spice island of Jamaica, has sadly become a factory-made clone, but made at home it's dark, sticky, fragrant with ginger – the real thing.

175g plain flour, sifted ◆ 1 level tablespoon ground ginger ◆ 1 level dessertspoon ground cinnamon
¼ nutmeg, grated ◆ ½ level teaspoon bicarbonate of soda ◆ 2 tablespoons milk
75g black treacle ◆ 75g golden syrup ◆ 75g dark brown soft sugar ◆ 75g block butter
1 large egg, lightly beaten

A Silverwood loaf tin (or a standard 2lb loaf tin),
lined with a 2lb traditional loaf tin liner (see page 16)

Pre-heat the oven to 170°C, gas mark 3

Begin by placing the tin of black treacle (without a lid) in a saucepan of barely simmering water to warm it and make it easier to measure (see page 78). Sift the flour and spices into a large bowl, then mix the bicarbonate of soda with the milk and set it on one side. Now measure the black treacle, golden syrup, sugar and butter into a saucepan with 75ml of water, heat and gently stir until thoroughly melted and blended – don't let it come anywhere near the boil and don't go off and leave it!

Next add the syrup mixture to the flour and spices, beating vigorously with a wooden spoon, and when the mixture is smooth, beat in the egg a little at a time, followed by the bicarbonate of soda and milk. Now pour the mixture into the prepared tin and bake on a lower shelf so that the top of the tin is aligned with the centre of the oven for 1¼–1½ hours until it's well-risen and firm to the touch.

Remove the cake from the oven and allow to cool in the tin for 5 minutes before turning out. If possible, store it in a cake tin, still in its lining, for 24 hours before eating, and serve it cut in thick slices spread with butter.

STICKY TOFFEE LOAF CAKE
with FUDGE ICING

It's the dates (as in the famous pudding) that give this dark, sticky cake its toffee flavour, which is complemented beautifully by the fudge-flavoured icing.

*110g stoned dates ◆ 50g pecan nuts ◆ 110g spreadable butter ◆ 50g black treacle
175g golden syrup ◆ 150ml milk ◆ 2 large eggs ◆ 225g plain flour ◆ 1 level teaspoon mixed spice
2 level teaspoons ground ginger ◆ 1 level teaspoon bicarbonate of soda*

*For the icing: 4 tablespoons evaporated milk ◆ 3 tablespoons dark brown soft sugar
50g butter ◆ 150g golden icing sugar*

*A Silverwood loaf tin (or a standard 2lb loaf tin),
lined with a 2lb traditional loaf tin liner (see page 16)*

Pre-heat the oven to 150°C, gas mark 2

First place the tin of black treacle (without a lid) in a saucepan of barely simmering water to warm it and make it easier to measure (see page 78). Next prepare the dates and pecans. The nuts should be chopped fairly small and the dates should be chopped into equally small pieces.

Now to make the cake mixture: place the butter, black treacle and syrup in a large saucepan and melt them together over a gentle heat. Remove the mixture from the heat, let it cool for a few minutes, then mix in the milk.

Now beat the eggs and add those to the syrup mixture as well. Next sift the flour, spices and bicarbonate of soda into a bowl and gradually whisk the syrup mixture into the dry ingredients, bit by bit, until you have a smooth batter. Then lightly stir in the pecans and about two thirds of the dates, and pour the mixture into the prepared tin. Now lightly drop the rest of the dates on the top, pushing them gently in with a skewer. I find adding this amount of dates last of all gives a better distribution of fruit as the mixture is a fairly slack one.

Place the cake on a lower shelf so that the top of the tin is aligned with the centre of the oven and bake it for 1½ hours to 1 hour 50 minutes by which time it will have a very rounded, slightly cracked top. Cool it in the tin for about half an hour before turning it out.

To make the icing: in a small saucepan melt together the evaporated milk, brown sugar and butter, then simmer the mixture for 5 minutes. After that tip it into a bowl and leave it to cool. Then sift in the golden icing sugar and whisk everything together till smooth. Finally, using a palette knife, spread the icing all over the top of the cooled cake. Keep the cake in a tin in its liner – and it does seem to improve if kept for a couple of days before eating.

CARAWAY SEED CAKE

Dated? Old-fashioned? Maybe, but our tasters all gave it the thumbs-up and said please include it.

175g self-raising flour, sifted ◆ *175g spreadable butter* ◆ *175g golden caster sugar*
3 large eggs, beaten ◆ *50g ground almonds* ◆ *4 tablespoons milk*
3 rounded teaspoons caraway seeds

For the topping: *2 level tablespoons demerara sugar*
1 level tablespoon flaked almonds, crushed a bit

A Silverwood loaf tin (or a standard 2lb loaf tin),
lined with a 2lb traditional loaf tin liner (see page 16)
Pre-heat the oven to 180°C, gas mark 4

What you do is sift the flour into a roomy mixing bowl, lifting the sieve quite high to give the flour a good airing as it goes down, then simply add all the other ingredients. Now, using an electric hand whisk, combine them for about 1 minute until you have a smooth creamy consistency.

Spoon the mixture into the prepared tin. Level off the surface with the back of a spoon, then sprinkle the demerara sugar and crushed almonds all over. Bake on a lower shelf so that the top of the tin is aligned with the centre of the oven for about 1 hour 5 minutes, or until the cake is springy in the centre. Cool in the tin for 10 minutes, then turn out onto a wire rack to cool. I think that this cake tastes better after a day or two, so leave it in its liner and store in a tin.

MADEIRA CAKE

A bit of a plain Jane, you might think. But we still all love it. There are times when
a piece of really good plain cake is all you want. In this case I would choose to serve it with
a glass of chilled Madeira wine, which is in fact what it was invented for.

225g plain flour ◆ pinch of salt ◆ 2 level teaspoons baking powder
175g spreadable butter ◆ 2 large eggs, beaten ◆ 110g golden caster sugar
grated zest of 1 large lemon ◆ 2–3 tablespoons milk (to mix)
1 thin slice candied citron peel (optional)

A Silverwood loaf tin (or a standard 2lb loaf tin),
lined with a 2lb traditional loaf tin liner (see page 16)
Pre-heat the oven to 170°C, gas mark 3

Start by sifting the flour, salt and baking powder into a roomy mixing bowl,
lifting the sieve quite high to give the flour a good airing as it goes down. Then simply add
the butter, eggs, sugar and grated zest and, using an electric hand whisk, combine them
for about 1 minute until you have a smooth consistency.

Then add the milk, a tablespoon at a time – you need enough to make a creamy consistency
that drops off a spoon easily when tapped on the side of the bowl. Be careful not to add too much milk –
it needs to be a little stiffer than a sponge cake mix. Now spoon the mixture into the loaf tin, levelling it
off with the back of a tablespoon, and bake on a lower shelf so that the top of the tin is aligned with the
centre of the oven for 1 hour or until it feels springy in the centre. Leave in the tin for 10 minutes
before turning out onto a wire rack to cool. Store in an airtight tin in its liner.

If you like to follow tradition you can lightly place a thin slice of candied citron peel
on the surface before baking.

APRICOT, APPLE & PECAN LOAF

Everyone loves this cake, which is rather special, full of good wholesome ingredients
and so easy to make. To ring the changes you could use soft prunes and walnuts in place of the
apricots and pecans, plus one rounded teaspoon of mixed spice.

175g pecan nuts ◆ 110g wholemeal flour ◆ 110g plain flour ◆ pinch of salt
1½ level teaspoons baking powder ◆ 2 rounded teaspoons ground cinnamon
110g spreadable butter ◆ 175g light brown soft sugar ◆ 2 large eggs, beaten
3 tablespoons milk (plus a little extra if needed)
175g ready-to-eat dried apricots, each chopped in half
175g Bramley apples, cored and cut into 1cm chunks with the skin on

For the topping: *2 level tablespoons demerara sugar, combined with ¼ teaspoon ground cinnamon*

A Silverwood loaf tin (or a standard 2lb loaf tin),
lined with a 2lb traditional loaf tin liner (see page 16)
Pre-heat the oven to 180°C, gas mark 4

First of all, when the oven has pre-heated, spread the nuts out on a baking sheet and
toast them lightly for about 8 minutes, using a timer so that you don't forget them. After that
remove them to a chopping board, let them cool a bit, then chop them roughly.

Meanwhile take a large mixing bowl and sift the two flours, salt, baking powder and
cinnamon into it, holding the sieve up high to give the flour a good airing (adding the bran
from the sieve to the bowl as well). Then simply add the rest of the ingredients except the fruit
and nuts. Using an electric hand whisk, begin to beat the mixture on a slow speed, then
increase the speed to mix everything thoroughly till smooth.

Lightly fold in the apricots, apples and pecans. When everything's folded in, add a
drop more milk if necessary to give a mixture that drops easily off the spoon when you give it a
sharp tap. Pile the mixture into the lined tin, level the top with the back of a tablespoon and
sprinkle on the cinnamon sugar.

Bake the loaf on a lower shelf so the top of the tin is aligned with the centre of the
oven for about an hour, then cover loosely with a piece of foil and leave to bake for a further
15–30 minutes or until the cake feels springy in the centre. When it's cooked, remove it from the
oven and allow to cool for about 5 minutes before turning it out onto a wire cooling rack,
leaving it in its liner. Let it get completely cold before transferring to a cake tin.

Family Cakes

FAMILY CAKE

Nothing very trendy or sexy here. We thought maybe time had moved on. But we
were so wrong. This cake has a charm all of its own, top votes from tasters and fits the bill for everything
– packed lunches, picnics or just a little treat with a cup of tea or coffee.

275g self-raising flour ◆ 1 rounded teaspoon baking powder ◆ 225g spreadable butter
225g caster sugar ◆ 4 large eggs ◆ a few drops almond extract ◆ 110g mixed dried fruit
25g natural glacé cherries, sliced ◆ 1½ level tablespoons demerara sugar ◆ 50g flaked almonds

A buttered Silverwood oblong tin 20cm by 26cm, 4cm deep,
with a liner (see page 13)
Pre-heat the oven to 180°C, gas mark 4

First of all sift the flour and baking powder into a roomy mixing bowl, lifting the sieve
quite high to give the flour a good airing as it goes down. Then simply add the butter, caster sugar,
eggs and almond extract. Now, using an electric hand whisk, combine them for about 1 minute
until you have a smooth creamy consistency. Next fold in the dried fruits and cherries.

Spoon the mixture into the prepared tin, spreading it out evenly with the back of a tablespoon, then
sprinkle the surface of the cake with the demerara sugar and flaked almonds and bake near the
centre of the oven for about 40–50 minutes or until the centre feels springy to the touch. Leave in
the tin to cool for 10 minutes before turning out. Store in an airtight tin. Serve cut into squares.

ICED HONEY & SPICE CAKE

This is another cake that has a unique and different combination of punchy flavours – which makes it good for eating out-of-doors. Great for a picnic or afternoon tea in the garden.

225g plain flour ◆ 1 level teaspoon ground ginger ◆ 1 level teaspoon ground cinnamon
¼ teaspoon ground cloves ◆ 75g caster sugar ◆ zest of 1 small orange and 1 small lemon
110g block butter ◆ 1 large egg, beaten ◆ 75g clear, runny honey
1 level teaspoon bicarbonate of soda ◆ 50g mixed candied peel, finely chopped

For the icing: 175g sifted fondant icing sugar ◆ 4–6 teaspoons lemon juice

To decorate: 8 pieces of crystallised ginger

An 18cm round loose-based tin, base lined (see page 13) and lightly buttered
Pre-heat the oven to 170°C, gas mark 3

First of all place a small bowl in a saucepan containing barely simmering water and warm the honey a little – but be careful, it mustn't be too hot, just warm. Next sift the flour and spices into a large mixing bowl, then add the sugar and the orange and lemon zest. Now add the butter in small pieces and rub it lightly into the flour, using your fingertips, until the mixture becomes crumbly.

Next, lightly mix in the beaten egg using a large fork, followed by the warm honey. In a small basin mix the bicarbonate of soda with 3 tablespoons of cold water, stir until dissolved, then add it to the cake mixture and beat, quite hard, until the mixture is smooth and soft. Finally, stir in the mixed peel and spoon the mixture into the prepared tin, spreading it out evenly with the back of the spoon. Bake the cake near the centre of the oven for about 30–40 minutes or until well-risen and springy to touch. Cool it for about 10 minutes, then turn it out onto a wire rack to get quite cold (see page 12).

Meanwhile prepare the icing by sifting the icing sugar into a bowl, then add the lemon juice gradually, stirring well with a wooden spoon until the mixture coats the back of the spoon. Pour the icing all over, letting it run down slightly at the sides. Then decorate the top with the pieces of ginger and store in a tin until needed.

OLD-FASHIONED CHERRY CAKE

OK. It is an old-fashioned, very English kind of cake, and yes the cherries sometimes sink but believe me there are many people who are still very attached to it. If you're one of these, we have found the old-fashioned creaming-block-butter method works best, and if you slice the cherries, fold in two thirds of them then simply poke in the other third just before it goes into the oven, they don't sink.

*200g glacé cherries ◆ 175g block butter, at room temperature ◆ 175g golden caster sugar
3 large eggs, whisked lightly ◆ 175g plain flour ◆ ½ level teaspoon baking powder
75g ground almonds ◆ a few drops almond extract ◆ 1 dessertspoon milk*

*An 18cm round cake tin, buttered and with base and sides lined (see page 13)
Pre-heat the oven to 180°C, gas mark 4*

Begin by preparing the cherries. If they're dripping in syrup, pat them dry with kitchen paper, then slice each one into four. For the cake, cream the butter and sugar together until light, pale and fluffy. Now gradually beat in the whisked eggs a little at a time.

Then sift the flour and baking powder together, and carefully fold this into the creamed mixture using a metal spoon. Toss two thirds of the cherries together with the ground almonds and carefully fold these into the cake, adding one or two drops of almond extract and the milk.

Now spoon the cake mix into the prepared tin, level off the top with the back of a spoon, then sprinkle over the remaining third of the cherries and poke them just under the surface with a teaspoon.

Bake the cake near the centre of the oven for 50 minutes, then cover with foil and continue cooking for a further 10 minutes, or until the centre is springy to touch. Cool the cake in the tin for 15 minutes before turning it out onto a wire rack to cool. Store in an airtight tin.

CHUNKY APPLE CAKE

Apples are superb in cakes, so in the autumn when there are lots of windfalls around,
why not make a few of these and freeze them.

225g self-raising flour ◆ 1 rounded teaspoon baking powder ◆ 1 level teaspoon mixed spice
½ level teaspoon ground cinnamon ◆ 3 Bramley apples (about 550g)
2 large eggs, beaten ◆ 75g spreadable butter ◆ 175g light brown soft sugar
grated zest of 1 large orange ◆ 1 tablespoon chopped mixed peel
1 tablespoon milk (if needed) ◆ a little icing sugar

A 20cm loose-based round tin, buttered and base lined (see page 13)
Pre-heat the oven to 180°C, gas mark 4

Begin by sifting the flour, baking powder and spices into a roomy mixing bowl,
lifting the sieve quite high to give the flour a good airing as it goes down. Next chop the
apples into small dice (with or without peel, just as you like). Then place them in a
bowl and toss them with one tablespoon of the sieved flour mixture.

Then add the eggs, butter and sugar to the rest of the flour, and using an electric
hand whisk, combine them for about 1 minute until you have a smooth creamy consistency.
After that fold in the grated orange zest, mixed peel and diced apple.

If the mixture seems a little dry, add a tablespoon of milk. Now spoon the cake
mix into the prepared tin and level it off with the back of a spoon. Then bake near the centre
of the oven for about one hour or until the cake feels springy in the centre when lightly
pressed with a fingertip and just shows signs of shrinking away from the edge of the tin.
Cool in the tin for 10 minutes before turning out onto a wire rack (see page 12). This looks
nice dusted with sifted icing sugar just before serving. Store in an airtight tin.

FLAPJACKS

MAKES 16

There has been a bit of toing and froing on this one, and a fifty-fifty split among our tasters.
Some like them richer and very buttery, some like them drier and with a bit more crunch.
I prefer the latter, but here you can make your own choice.

150g soft brown sugar ◆ 225g or 275g block butter (see above)
1 rounded tablespoon golden syrup ◆ 350g porridge oats

A Silverwood oblong tin 20cm by 26cm, 4cm deep, with a liner (see page 13)
Pre-heat the oven to 150°C, gas mark 2

First place the sugar, butter and golden syrup together in a saucepan and heat it gently
until the butter has melted, giving it a stir now and then. Take the saucepan off the heat and stir in
the porridge oats, mixing thoroughly. Now pour the mixture into the prepared tin and press it
out evenly, using the back of a tablespoon or your hand.

Bake near the centre of the oven for 40–45 minutes. Then allow the mixture to cool in
the tin for 10 minutes before cutting into oblong bars. Leave them in the tin until they're quite
cold before removing them to store in an airtight tin.

For chocolate-dipped flapjacks: use 110g melted milk chocolate (for children) or dark
chocolate (for adults) in a wide bowl, and dip them lengthways 5mm deep into the chocolate
(just to cover one side). See the Florentine recipe on page 150 for how to melt chocolate.

TRADITIONAL OATMEAL PARKIN

But which tradition is it? My grandparents claimed Yorkshire emphatically, while my Lancashire friends are just as emphatic. Either way I just love it, and because it's so easy to make, if you haven't yet tasted parkin I urge you to try it. Its virtue is it keeps well and goes on getting stickier. We use a pleated silicone liner in the tin, which helps keep the moisture in during storage.

225g golden syrup ◆ 50g black treacle ◆ 110g block butter ◆ 110g dark brown soft sugar
225g medium oatmeal ◆ 110g self-raising flour ◆ 2 level teaspoons ground ginger
pinch of salt ◆ 1 large egg, beaten ◆ 1 tablespoon milk

An 18cm loose-based round cake tin, with a pleated silicone (see page 16) liner
Pre-heat the oven to 140°C, gas mark 1

To weigh syrup and treacle, it helps to place the opened tins in a pan of barely simmering water for 5 minutes to make them easier to pour. Then weigh a saucepan on the scales, and weigh the syrup and treacle into it. Now add the butter and the sugar to the saucepan and place it over a gentle heat until the butter has melted – don't go away and leave it unattended, because for this you don't want it to boil.

Meanwhile measure the oatmeal, flour and ginger into a mixing bowl, add a pinch of salt, then gradually stir in the warmed syrup mixture till everything is thoroughly blended. Next add the beaten egg and, lastly, the milk. Now pour the mixture into the prepared tin and bake near the centre shelf of the oven for 1½ hours. Then cool the parkin in the tin for 30 minutes before turning out. Don't worry if it sinks slightly in the middle – this is quite normal. When it's completely cold, store in an airtight tin.

DAMP GINGERBREAD

There has been much debate about the title of this recipe. 'Damp' is not the usual adjective to describe a cake, but a recent group of tasters nodded in assent – it does kind of say it. Its texture is quite different from other cakes, so taste some and see what you think.

350g golden syrup ◆ 125g block butter ◆ 250g plain flour, sifted ◆ ½ level teaspoon salt
1¾ level teaspoons bicarbonate of soda ◆ 1 level tablespoon ground ginger
½ level teaspoon mixed spice ◆ 1 large egg ◆ 275ml milk

To make this you'll need a Silverwood oblong tin 20cm by 26cm, 4cm deep,
well buttered and with a liner (see page 13)
Pre-heat the oven to 180°C, gas mark 4

First weigh out the syrup into a small saucepan (see page 78). Then add the butter to the saucepan and melt the two together over a gentle heat. Meanwhile measure the dry ingredients into a bowl, then gradually pour in the syrup mixture, mixing thoroughly.

Now beat the egg and milk together in a separate basin then add that bit by bit, again mixing very thoroughly. The cake batter will seem very liquid at this stage but that's quite normal so don't worry, just pour it into the prepared tin and bake near the centre of the oven for about 50 minutes or until the centre is springy. Cool in the tin for 5 minutes before turning out onto a wire tray to cool. When it's cold, cut it into squares and store in an airtight tin.

PRESERVED GINGER CAKE

MAKES 15 SQUARES

In the original book, and ever since, this has been one of my own top favourites, and has been hugely popular with everyone. But this time round we have used the all-in-one method, so it's much easier, and we've discovered the whole thing freezes beautifully for up to a month.

225g self-raising flour ◆ 1 slightly rounded teaspoon baking powder ◆ 175g spreadable butter
175g golden caster sugar ◆ 3 large eggs ◆ 1 tablespoon black treacle
1 level dessertspoon ground ginger ◆ 2 tablespoons milk ◆ 1 heaped tablespoon ground almonds
2 tablespoons ginger syrup (from the preserved ginger) ◆ 7 pieces preserved stem ginger

For the icing and topping: 225g white fondant icing sugar ◆ juice of 1 large lemon

To make this you'll need a Silverwood oblong tin 20cm by 26cm, 4cm deep,
buttered and with a liner (see page 13)
Pre-heat the oven to 170°C, gas mark 3

Begin by placing the opened tin of black treacle in a saucepan of barely simmering water to warm it and make it easier to spoon. Meanwhile sift the flour and baking powder into a roomy mixing bowl, lifting the sieve quite high to give the flour a good airing as it goes down, then add the butter, golden caster sugar, eggs, treacle and ground ginger. Now, using an electric hand whisk, combine them for about 1 minute until you have a smooth creamy consistency.

After that fold in the milk, along with the heaped tablespoon of ground almonds and the ginger syrup. Then chop 5 of the pieces of stem ginger fairly small and fold these into the cake mix too. Spread the cake mix in the tin, level it off with the back of a tablespoon and bake for 40–50 minutes near the centre of the oven or until the cake is risen, springy and firm to the touch in the centre. Leave to cool in the tin for 10 minutes, then lift the cake out of the tin using the liner and place it on a wire rack. Then, holding the liner at one end, use a palette knife to slide the cake directly onto the rack, and leave until cold.

For the icing: sift the icing sugar into a bowl and mix with enough lemon juice to make the consistency of thin cream. Spread the icing over the top of the cake, and never mind if it dribbles down the side in a few places – it looks nice and homemade. Cut the remaining 2 pieces of stem ginger into 15 pieces and arrange in lines of three across the cake. For serving, cut the cake into 15 squares.

TRADITIONAL DUNDEE CAKE

There are a million and one versions of Dundee cake, so please don't write to me and say this isn't the real one! What I can guarantee is that this is a beautiful cake. It's not rich and moist like a Christmas cake, but lighter and more crumbly in texture.

225g plain flour ◆ 1 level teaspoon baking powder ◆ 50g spreadable butter
150g golden caster sugar ◆ 3 large eggs ◆ 1 dessertspoon milk (if needed) ◆ 175g currants
175g sultanas ◆ 50g glacé cherries, rinsed, dried, and cut into halves
50g mixed candied peel, finely chopped ◆ 2 level tablespoons ground almonds
grated zest of 1 orange and 1 lemon

For the topping: 60g whole blanched almonds

An 18cm loose-based round tin, buttered with base and side lined (see page 13)
Pre-heat the oven to 170°C, gas mark 3

First of all sift the flour and baking powder into a roomy mixing bowl, lifting the sieve quite high to give the flour a good airing as it goes down. Then simply add the butter, caster sugar and eggs, and, using an electric hand whisk, combine them for about 1–2 minutes until you have a smooth dropping consistency. If it seems too dry, add a dessertspoon of milk.

Next fold in all the other ingredients: currants, sultanas, cherries, mixed peel, ground almonds and orange and lemon zest. Now spoon the mixture into the prepared cake tin, spreading it out evenly with the back of the spoon. Then, carefully, arrange the whole almonds in concentric circles over the top – but drop them on very lightly (if you press them down too hard they will disappear during the cooking). Place the cake near the centre of the oven and bake for 1¾ hours or until the centre is firm and springy to touch. Allow it to cool before taking it out of the tin. Dundee cake keeps very well in an airtight tin and tastes better if it's kept a few days before cutting.

STICKY PRUNE & DATE CAKE

An unequivocal winner! Dark, sticky, very moist, keeps like a dream, has always been hugely popular with everyone who makes it.

175g dates, stoned and chopped ◆ 125g ready-to-eat prunes, chopped ◆ 75g raisins
75g currants ◆ 200g block butter ◆ 200ml water ◆ 300g condensed milk
110g plain flour ◆ 110g wholemeal flour ◆ pinch of salt ◆ ½ level teaspoon bicarbonate of soda
1 rounded tablespoon chunky marmalade

For the glaze: 1½ tablespoons marmalade ◆ ½ tablespoon water

A 20cm round loose-based cake tin, base and side lined (see page 13)
Pre-heat the oven to 170°C, gas mark 3

Begin by placing all the fruits, the butter, water and condensed milk in a saucepan, then simply bring it to the boil, stirring quite frequently to prevent it sticking. Let the mixture simmer for 3 minutes exactly – still stirring occasionally and, whatever you do, don't forget it! Now transfer the mixture to a large mixing bowl, to cool off for about 30 minutes.

While it's cooling, weigh out the flours, then sift them onto a plate, adding the salt and bicarbonate of soda. (When you sieve wholemeal flour there are usually some bits of bran left in the sieve, so just tip them back into the rest of the sieved flour.) When the fruit mixture has cooled, stir the flour, salt and bicarbonate of soda into it, adding a nice round tablespoon of marmalade too.

Then spoon the mixture into the prepared tin, level it off with the back of a tablespoon and bake the cake on a lower shelf so that the top of the tin is aligned with the centre of the oven for 1 hour and 50 minutes. Have a look halfway through, and if the top of the cake looks a bit dark put a double square of baking parchment on top to protect it. Then let the cake cool in the tin for 5 minutes before turning it out to cool on a wire tray.

When the cake is completely cold, gently heat the marmalade in a small saucepan with the water. Then brush it all over the top of the cake. Store in an airtight tin.

DOUBLE LEMON DRIZZLE CAKE
with POPPY SEEDS

This is the definitive Lemon Drizzle cake, and we have used four lemons. There's almost as much drizzle as cake, so after you bite through the crunchy crust it is very lemony and syrupy inside.

175g self-raising flour ◆ *1 teaspoon baking powder* ◆ *175g spreadable butter*
175g golden caster sugar ◆ *3 large eggs* ◆ *grated zest of 3 large lemons*
juice of 1 large lemon ◆ *40g poppy seeds*

For the syrup: juice of 3 large lemons ◆ *grated zest of 1 large lemon*
50g golden icing sugar, sifted ◆ *100g golden granulated sugar*

To finish: 1 rounded tablespoon golden granulated sugar,
mixed with 1 rounded teaspoon poppy seeds

A 20cm loose-based round cake tin, greased and base lined (see page 13)
Pre-heat the oven to 170°C, gas mark 3

Start off by sifting the flour and baking powder into a roomy mixing bowl, holding the sieve quite high to give the flour a good airing as it goes down. Then add the butter, sugar, eggs, lemon zest and juice and finally the poppy seeds. Now, using an electric hand whisk, mix to a smooth creamy consistency for about one minute. Spoon the mixture into the tin, levelling it with the back of the spoon, and bake near the centre of the oven for 40 minutes or until the centre feels springy.

When the cake is ready, remove the tin from the oven to a board, then straight away mix together the syrup ingredients. Next stab the cake all over with a skewer and spoon the syrup evenly over the hot cake, then finally sprinkle with the sugar and poppy seed mixture. After that the cake needs to cool in its tin before it can be removed (see page 12) and stored in an airtight container.

Note: this is equally good made without the poppy seeds if you prefer.

Little Cakes

CHOCOLATE 'SURPRISE' CUP CAKES

MAKES 12

It's the hidden ingredient that's the surprise. Mashed potato, often used in potato scones but even better in these small cakes – giving them a soft moist texture. I find frozen mashed potato works really well for this. For children you may like to leave the spice out, but I know a five-year-old who loves the subtle spiciness.

75g dark chocolate (minimum 70% cocoa solids) ◆ 50g condensed milk
50g light muscovado sugar ◆ 75g block butter
110g mashed potato (can be frozen and defrosted)
110g sifted self-raising flour ◆ 1 level teaspoon baking powder ◆ 1 large egg
1 level teaspoon Chinese five spice powder

For a dark chocolate icing: 50g dark chocolate ◆ 100g condensed milk
10g block butter ◆ 24 pink chocolate buttons

Or for a milk chocolate topping: 75g milk chocolate (minimum 30% cocoa powder)
75g condensed milk ◆ 10g block butter ◆ 24 white chocolate buttons

Or for a white chocolate topping: 75g white chocolate ◆ 75g condensed milk
10g block butter ◆ 24 milk chocolate buttons

Two Silverwood 6-cup muffin trays, lined with paper fairy cake cases (see page 16)
Pre-heat the oven to 180°C, gas mark 4

Begin by placing the chocolate, broken up, in a medium heatproof bowl, then add the condensed milk, sugar and butter. Place this over a saucepan of barely simmering water, making sure the bowl does not touch the water. Then, keeping the heat at its lowest, leave everything to melt slowly, giving it the odd stir. It should take about 6 minutes for everything to combine and melt.

Meanwhile place the remaining cake ingredients in a large bowl and when the chocolate mixture is ready, add it to the rest and whisk it in until everything is smooth and creamy. Now divide the mixture between the paper cases and bake them near the centre of the oven for about 15 minutes. After that allow them to cool in the tin, and while that's happening make your chosen icing.

Just put the chocolate and condensed milk into another heatproof bowl and melt together (as above). Then take the bowl off the heat, stir in the butter until melted and allow the mixture to cool for about 5 minutes. Using a small palette knife, spread the mixture over the top of the cakes and finish each one with two chocolate buttons. Store in an airtight tin.

ORANGE CURD BUTTERFLY CAKES
MAKES 12

Still flying, in our opinion, and much loved by children and adults who can still
remember life before cup cakes.

175g self-raising flour, sifted ◆ *110g spreadable butter* ◆ *110g golden caster sugar*
2 large eggs ◆ *1 dessertspoon orange juice* ◆ *zest of 1 large orange*

For the orange curd filling: *finely grated zest and juice of 1 medium orange*
juice of ½ lemon ◆ *40g golden caster sugar* ◆ *2 large eggs* ◆ *50g block butter*

To serve: *A dusting of icing sugar*

Two Silverwood 6-cup muffin trays, lined with paper fairy cake cases
Pre-heat the oven to 190ºC, gas mark 5

Start by making the filling. Put the first four ingredients for the curd in a bowl
and whisk together. Then add the butter, cut into lumps, and fit the bowl over a pan of
simmering water. Now take a mini-whisk and whisk from time to time until the curd thickens –
about 10 minutes. Then remove the bowl and leave the curd to get quite cold.

To make the cakes, combine all the ingredients together in a bowl and, using an electric whisk,
beat until absolutely smooth (1–2 minutes). Then drop an equal quantity of the mixture into the
paper cases and bake near the centre of the oven for 15–20 minutes or until the cakes
are well-risen and golden. Then remove them to a wire rack and leave to cool.

To fill the cakes, angle a small sharp knife and cut to within about 1cm of the
edge of each cake to remove a cone-shaped round, leaving a cavity in the centre. Cut the
round in half and set aside. Now fill the centre of each cake with the curd and return
the two pieces of cake to sit on top like butterfly wings. Finally dust the cakes
with sifted icing sugar and store in an airtight tin.

WINNERS' CUP CAKES

MAKES 12

We make birthday cakes for children's parties at the football club that look like
football pitches, shirts etc. But for us at home these little cakes, made in football colours,
are simple and much appreciated by small football fans.

175g self-raising flour ◆ pinch of salt ◆ 110g spreadable butter
110g golden caster sugar ◆ 2 large eggs ◆ 1 teaspoon vanilla extract

For the icing: 150g fondant icing sugar, sifted
concentrated colouring pastes or powders

Two Silverwood 6-cup muffin trays, lined with paper muffin cases (see page 16)
Pre-heat the oven to 190ºC, gas mark 5

All you do is sift the flour into a roomy mixing bowl, lifting the sieve quite high
to give the flour a good airing as it goes down, then simply add all the other ingredients.
Now, using an electric hand whisk, combine them for about 1 minute until you have a smooth
creamy consistency. Next divide the mixture between the muffin cases. Then bake
the cakes near the centre of the oven for 20–25 minutes.

When the cakes are cooked (i.e. well-risen and golden), remove them to a wire
cooling tray to cool. Now for the icing: sift the icing sugar into a bowl and just add enough
cold water, a teaspoonful at a time, until you have a spreadable consistency. Using a cocktail stick,
add minute amounts of your chosen colour paste until you get the shade you want.

When the cakes are cold, use a small palette knife to spread the icing on top of each cake.
Now you need to leave the icing to set a bit (for about 30 minutes) and, if you like, pop
in a football flag (see page 224 for stockists).

ICED HIDDEN STRAWBERRY
CUP CAKES

MAKES 12

After the football cakes we felt we needed a very girly alternative – and these
really fit the bill. The cakes are pretty and delicate. Inside each is a hidden strawberry to bite into,
and to add to that the 'icing on the cake' is made with a strawberry purée.

*175g self-raising flour ◆ pinch of salt ◆ 110g spreadable butter ◆ 110g golden caster sugar
2 large eggs ◆ 1 teaspoon vanilla extract ◆ 12 smallish strawberries, hulled*

*For the icing: 50g strawberries, hulled ◆ 175g fondant icing sugar, sifted
a little extra icing sugar (to dust) ◆ 3 extra strawberries, quartered (to decorate)*

*Two Silverwood 6-cup muffin trays, and silver paper-lined fairy cake cases (see page 16)
Pre-heat the oven to 190ºC, gas mark 5*

All you do is sift the flour into a roomy mixing bowl, lifting the sieve quite high to
give the flour a good airing as it goes down, then simply add all the other ingredients (except
the strawberries). Now, using an electric hand whisk, combine them for about 1 minute
until you have a smooth creamy consistency.

Next, divide half the mixture between the cake cases, then place a strawberry
(pointed part uppermost) on top of each one. After that divide the remaining mixture between
the cases – making sure the strawberries are covered. Then bake the cakes near the centre
of the oven for 15–20 minutes.

While that's happening, make the strawberry icing. All you need to do is whizz
the strawberries to a purée in a mini-chopper, then sieve the purée into a bowl containing the
icing sugar, mixing as you go. You may not need all the purée, just enough to give it a good
spreadable consistency. Cover the bowl with some damp kitchen paper.

When the cakes are cooked (i.e. well-risen and golden), remove them to a wire cooling
tray, and when they're cold, use a small palette knife to spread the icing on top of each cake.
You need to leave the icing to set for about 30 minutes. Then top each one with a quarter of a
strawberry and finish off with a dusting of icing sugar. These are best eaten as fresh as possible.

WELSH CAKES

MAKES ABOUT 20

These have been a huge success with everyone who has tasted them, and because
they're cooked on top of the stove, children (with supervision) love making them. Serve them
warm with lots of butter, and later on they're very good toasted.

225g self-raising flour ◆ 1 level teaspoon mixed spice ◆ 75g caster sugar
110g spreadable butter ◆ 110g mixed dried fruit ◆ 1 large egg
a little milk (if needed) ◆ a little extra butter

A good solid frying pan with a flat base, plus a 6.5cm plain round cutter

First sift the dry ingredients together, and rub in the butter until the mixture is coarsely
crumbled. Then add the fruit and mix it in thoroughly. Now beat the egg lightly and add it to the
mixture. Mix to a dough and, if it seems a little too dry, add just a spot of milk.

Now transfer the dough onto a lightly floured working surface and roll it out with a
floured rolling pin to about 5mm thick. Then, using the cutter, cut the dough into rounds
by giving it a sharp tap (and avoid twisting it), re-rolling the trimmings until all the dough
is used. Next, lightly grease the pan, using a piece of kitchen paper smeared with butter.

Heat the pan over a medium heat and cook the Welsh cakes for about 3 minutes on
each side. If they look as if they're browning too quickly, turn the heat down a bit because it's
important to cook them through – but they should be fairly brown and crisp on the outside.
Serve them warm, with lots of butter and homemade jam or perhaps some Welsh honey.

RICH FRUIT SCONES

MAKES ABOUT 8

These don't need clotted cream and preserves – just serve them fresh and warm from the oven with a serious amount of really good butter.

225g self-raising flour ◆ 40g golden caster sugar ◆ 75g spreadable butter
50g mixed dried fruit ◆ 1 large egg, beaten ◆ about 3–4 tablespoons milk (to mix)
a little extra flour

A baking sheet with a non-stick liner, and a 5cm plain (or fluted) cutter
Pre-heat the oven to 220°C, gas mark 7

First sift the flour into a bowl then add the sugar and rub the butter into the dry ingredients until the mixture looks crumbly. Now sprinkle in the dried fruit, pour in the beaten egg and add 3 tablespoons of milk. Start to mix to a dough with a knife, then bring the mixture together using your hands – it should be a soft but not a sticky dough, so add more milk (a teaspoon at a time) if the dough seems too dry.

Form the dough into a ball and turn it out onto a lightly floured working surface. Now, with a floured rolling pin, roll it out very lightly to a thickness of about 3cm. (This thickness is vital. The reason scones don't rise enough is because they are rolled too thin.) Then take the pastry cutter and tap it sharply so that it goes straight through the dough – do not twist or the scones will turn out a strange shape!

When you have cut as many as you can, knead the remaining dough together again and repeat. Then place the scones on the baking sheet, dust each one with flour and bake near the top of the oven for 12–15 minutes. When they're done they will have risen and turned a golden brown. Remove them to a cooling tray and serve very fresh, split and spread with butter.

PLAIN SCONES

MAKES ABOUT 8

Plain, meaning without added fruit, but light, airy and just the right amount of crusty surface makes these scones the perfect backdrop to preserves and clotted cream. You can make them with buttermilk and natural yoghurt in place of the milk, and you can use 1 level teaspoon of bicarbonate of soda and 2 level teaspoons of cream of tartar with plain flour if you want to experiment, but the recipe below seems equally good to us and the ingredients are always available.

40g spreadable butter ◆ 225g self-raising flour, sieved
1½ level tablespoons golden caster sugar ◆ pinch of salt
110ml milk, plus a little more (if needed) ◆ a little extra flour

A baking sheet with a non-stick liner, and a 5cm plain (or fluted) cutter
Pre-heat the oven to 220°C, gas mark 7

Begin by rubbing the butter into the sieved flour quickly, using your fingertips, then stir in the sugar followed by a pinch of salt. Now, using a knife, mix in the milk little by little, and when it's all in, flour your hands and knead the mixture to a soft dough (you may find you need just a drop more milk if it feels at all dry).

Place the dough on a floured pastry board and with a rolling pin (also floured) lightly roll it out to a thickness of about 3cm. (This thickness is vital. The reason scones don't rise enough is because they are rolled too thin.) Then take the pastry cutter and tap it sharply so that it goes straight through the dough – do not twist or the scones will turn out a strange shape!

When you have cut as many as you can, knead the remaining dough together again and repeat. Then place the scones on the baking sheet, dust each one with flour and bake near the top of the oven for 12–15 minutes. When they're done they will have risen and turned a golden brown. Then transfer them to a wire rack and eat as soon as they are cool enough, spread with butter, jam and clotted cream.

VIENNESE TARTLETS

MAKES 12

The texture of these is not like anything else. They are very short and buttery,
and seem to just melt in the mouth. We like them filled with morello cherry jam because by
contrast it's not too sweet.

175g spreadable butter ◆ *60g icing sugar, sifted* ◆ *1 teaspoon vanilla extract*
150g self-raising flour, sieved ◆ *40g cornflour*
4 tablespoons morello cherry jam (or any other) ◆ *extra icing sugar (to dust)*

Two Silverwood 6-cup muffin trays, lined with paper fairy cake cases (see page 16)
Pre-heat the oven to 180°C, gas mark 4

Start off by beating the butter, icing sugar and vanilla extract together with a
wooden spoon until very soft and creamy and then stir in the sieved flour and cornflour to form a
soft paste. Then divide the mixture between the paper cases. Using the back of a teaspoon dipped
briefly in water, make a space in the centre of each one to about two thirds of the way down
(so that you end up with a deep tartlet case).

Bake the cakes near the centre of the oven for 20 minutes until golden brown –
they will still be just slightly soft in the centre but don't worry about that. Cool in the tins
for 15 minutes, leaving them in their paper cases.

Now fill the centre of each tartlet with jam and leave to finish cooling. Just before serving sift
a light dusting of icing sugar over the top of each one. It doesn't matter if the icing sugar
obscures the jam – it will soon be absorbed so you'll end up with delicious little red blobs in
the centre. Store in an airtight tin.

GOOD OLD ROCK CAKES

MAKES 10–12

These were once economy cakes, not too expensive, providing cake for large families. They were not going to be included in this edition – until, that is, we made some. And unbelievably they went down a storm. Perhaps we've got so used to bland shop-bought stuff that even something as simple as this tastes so very good.

350g plain flour ◆ ¼ teaspoon salt ◆ 2 level teaspoons baking powder
175g light brown sugar ◆ about ¼ nutmeg, freshly grated ◆ ½ level teaspoon mixed spice
175g spreadable butter ◆ 125g mixed dried fruit ◆ 1 large egg
1–2 tablespoons milk (if needed)

A large baking sheet, lined with a non-stick liner (see page 13)
Pre-heat the oven to 190°C, gas mark 5

Mix the flour, salt, baking powder and sugar in a bowl, making sure you get all the little lumps out of the sugar, then add the spices and rub in the butter until the mixture looks like fine breadcrumbs. Lastly, stir in the fruit.

Now break the egg into a separate bowl and whisk it lightly with a fork, then add it to the flour mixture. Stir until the mixture forms a stiff dough (you may need to add a tablespoon of milk, though certainly not more than two). Now, using two forks, pile the mixture in irregular spiky heaps on the baking sheet. Bake near the centre of the oven for 18–20 minutes or until golden brown, then leave to cool for a minute on the tray before removing to a wire rack. Store in an airtight tin.

SPICED DATE & SESAME CRUNCHIES

MAKES ABOUT 18

The original recipe didn't have sesame seeds, which is an added dimension, and we're pleased they're popular with children since they're so easy to pop into a lunchbox.

225g dates, stoned and chopped ◆ 4 tablespoons water ◆ 1 tablespoon lemon juice
1 level teaspoon ground cinnamon ◆ 175g self-raising flour ◆ 175g semolina
175g block butter ◆ 75g demerara sugar ◆ 2 tablespoons sesame seeds

A Silverwood Swiss roll tin 20cm by 30cm, greased
Pre-heat the oven to 190°C, gas mark 5

Put the chopped dates, water, lemon juice and cinnamon in a small saucepan and heat gently, stirring occasionally, until the mixture looks as though it will spread fairly easily. Then take the saucepan off the heat and leave it to cool.

While it's cooling, mix the flour, semolina and sesame seeds together in a bowl. Now place the butter and sugar together in another small saucepan and heat gently until the butter has completely melted; then stir this mixture into the flour and semolina. Mix well, and press half the mixture into the tin, using your hands to spread it as evenly as possible all over.

Next spread the date mixture carefully over this – again as evenly as possible – and after that top with the remaining flour and semolina mixture. This will by now have cooled a little and will probably be a bit crumbly, so just sprinkle it over the date mixture, pressing it down lightly all over. Now bake near the centre of the oven for 30 minutes, until the surface is tinged nicely golden brown. Then cool, cut into bars and serve, or store in a tin till needed.

ECCLES CAKES

MAKES 20

Eccles cakes are pastries really, but have always been referred to as cakes. Traditionally in Eccles they were served with Lancashire cheese and this has been revived in some of our smarter restaurants and served in place of dessert. I think a lump of Mrs Kirkham's Lancashire cheese and an Eccles cake on a journey or at a picnic really hits the spot.

450g all-butter puff pastry

For the filling: *50g block butter* ◆ *125g dark brown soft sugar* ◆ *150g currants*
50g chopped mixed peel ◆ *zest of 1 large orange* ◆ *1 level teaspoon ground allspice*
¼ nutmeg, freshly grated

For the topping: *1 egg white (to brush)* ◆ *2 level tablespoons golden granulated sugar*

Two large baking sheets, lined with non-stick liners (see page 13)
Pre-heat the oven to 200°C, gas mark 6

Begin by preparing the filling: melt the butter in a small saucepan, then take it off the heat and stir in all the other filling ingredients quite thoroughly, and leave it to cool.

Next place the pastry on a lightly floured surface. Roll it out to a rectangle 32cm by 40cm. Turn the rectangle lengthways in front of you and cut it into five 8cm strips and then cut the strips across into four, so that you end up with twenty 8cm squares.

Arrange heaped teaspoonfuls of the filling in the centre of each square, dampen the edge of each square of pastry with water, then turn the corners inwards and seal them together. Flip each Eccles cake the other way up so the seals are underneath, then just shape it into a round with your hands and roll them lightly with a rolling pin to approximately 7mm thick.

Place them all on the baking sheets, then using a sharp knife make three slashes across each one and finally brush them with egg white and sprinkle with sugar. Bake them in the oven, one sheet at a time, on a highish shelf for about 15 minutes or until golden brown. Then transfer them to a wire rack to cool. Store in an airtight tin.
They also freeze beautifully for up to a month.

APRICOT OAT SLICES

MAKES 15

The day we tested these lovely, oaty, chewy cakes, I took them to a football club board meeting, and they all disappeared in moments.

110g porridge oats ◆ 225g plain wholemeal flour ◆ 75g dark brown soft sugar
2 teaspoons ground cinnamon ◆ 150g block butter, melted

For the filling: 350g ready-to-eat dried apricots (or dried dates), chopped

A Silverwood oblong tin 20cm by 26cm, 4cm deep,
with a liner (see page 13)
Pre-heat the oven to 200°C, gas mark 6

First measure the dry ingredients into a bowl, then stir in the butter quite thoroughly. Next sprinkle half the mixture over the base of the tin and, using your hands, press and even it out to form a base without any gaps. Then arrange the filling carefully all over this. Sprinkle the rest of the mixture evenly over the filling and press this down firmly. Bake near the centre of the oven (or just above) for about 20–25 minutes until golden brown. Leave in the tin for 10 minutes, then cut into 15 squares, cool on a wire rack and store in an airtight tin.

Note: these can be made with the same quantity of any other fruit. I particularly like dates but these need to be simmered in 6 tablespoons of water for about 10 minutes in advance. Or you can use fresh fruits – plums are good.

Muffins

APRICOT CRUMBLE MUFFINS

MAKES 6 LARGE MUFFINS

I am openly and quite unashamedly mad about muffins. They are a doddle to make once you grasp it, and for me they upstage cup cakes by a mile – low in fat, fruity, soft, squidgy, light and airy. My only problem is deciding which ones I like best. You can make these with ready-to-eat dried apricots, but in the summer they are even better made with fresh.

150g plain flour ◆ ½ level teaspoon ground cinnamon ◆ 1 level dessertspoon baking powder
¼ teaspoon salt ◆ 1 large egg ◆ 40g dark brown soft sugar ◆ 120ml milk
50g block butter, melted and slightly cooled ◆ 1 teaspoon vanilla extract
150g ready-to-eat dried apricots, finely chopped ◆ 50g pecan nuts, roughly chopped

For the topping: 75g soft dark brown sugar ◆ 40g plain flour ◆ ½ teaspoon baking powder
½ teaspoon ground cinnamon ◆ 40g butter, melted ◆ 25g pecan nuts, chopped

A Silverwood muffin tray lined with 6 paper muffin cases (see page 16),
generously brushed with melted butter
Pre-heat the oven to 200ºC, gas mark 6

With muffins it's always a good idea to have everything weighed out and ready before you start

To make the crumble topping, mix the sugar, flour, baking powder and cinnamon together in a bowl. Stir in the melted butter with a fork, followed by the chopped nuts.

Next sift the flour, cinnamon, baking powder and salt into a bowl, lifting the sieve up high to give the flour a good airing. Now, in another bowl whisk together the egg, sugar, milk, melted butter and vanilla. Then return the dry ingredients to the sieve and sift them straight into the egg mixture. (This double sifting is crucial because we won't be doing much mixing.)

What you now need to do is take a large metal spoon and fold the dry ingredients quickly into the wet ones – the key word here is quickly (i.e. in about 15 seconds). What you mustn't do is beat or stir the mixture – just do the folding, and ignore the uneven appearance of the mixture because that's precisely what makes the muffins really light. Over-mixing is where people go wrong. Next, quickly fold in the finely chopped apricots and pecan nuts – again no stirring. Now divide the mixture between the muffin cases.

Then sprinkle the crumble mixture evenly over each muffin, and bake near the centre of the oven for 25–30 minutes until well-risen and golden brown. Remove the muffins from the oven and transfer to a wire cooling tray. Store in an airtight tin.

ICED LEMON & POPPY SEED MUFFINS

MAKES 4 LARGE MUFFINS

A friend asked 'Can you make iced poppy seed muffins as good as a famous coffee-shop chain?'
Answer, decidedly yes, but with add-ons. Much lighter, moister, much much more lemony
without all the additives. And guess what? One fifth of the price!

150g plain flour ◆ 1 level dessertspoon baking powder ◆ ¼ teaspoon salt
zest and juice of 3 lemons (reserve 1 tablespoon of juice for the icing) ◆ 25g poppy seeds
1 large egg ◆ 40g golden caster sugar ◆ 2 tablespoons milk
50g block butter, melted and cooled slightly

For the icing: 110g fondant icing sugar, sifted
3–4 teaspoons lemon juice

A Silverwood muffin tray lined with 4 paper muffin cases (see page 16),
generously brushed with melted butter
Pre-heat the oven to 200°C, gas mark 6

With muffins it's always a good idea to have everything weighed out and ready before you start

Begin by sifting the flour, baking powder and salt into a bowl, lifting the sieve up
high to give the flour a good airing. Then, in another bowl, whisk together the lemon juice and
zest, poppy seeds, egg, sugar, milk and melted butter. Now return the dry ingredients to the sieve
and sift them straight into the egg mixture. (This double sifting is crucial because
we won't be doing much mixing.)

What you now need to do is take a large metal spoon and fold the dry ingredients
into the wet ones – the key word here is quickly (i.e. in about 15 seconds). What you mustn't
do is beat or stir, just do the folding – ignore the uneven appearance of the mixture because it's
precisely this that makes the muffins really light. Over-mixing is where people go wrong.

Now divide the mixture between the muffin cases. Bake near the centre
of the oven for 25–30 minutes until well-risen and golden brown. Remove the muffins from
the oven and transfer them straight to a wire rack to cool.

When they're absolutely cold add enough of the reserved lemon juice, a
teaspoon at a time, to the icing sugar until you have a spreadable consistency. Then divide the
icing between the cooled muffins and smooth it over the tops with a small palette knife.
When set, store in an airtight tin.

CHUNKY MARMALADE MUFFINS

MAKES 6 LARGE MUFFINS

Imagine a cold, dark wintery morning, and you'd like to serve someone something really special for breakfast. Perhaps a birthday treat? Then look no further.

150g plain flour ◆ *1 level dessertspoon baking powder* ◆ *¼ teaspoon salt*
zest and juice of 1 large orange ◆ *1 heaped tablespoon ground almonds*
1 large egg ◆ *a little milk* ◆ *50g block butter, melted and cooled slightly*
225g chunky Seville orange marmalade

To finish: 2 heaped tablespoons marmalade, warmed

A Silverwood muffin tray lined with 6 paper muffin cases (see page 16),
generously brushed with melted butter
Pre-heat the oven to 200°C, gas mark 6

With muffins it's always a good idea to have everything weighed out and ready before you start. When you have measured the orange juice into a jug, you need 120ml so if you don't quite have that, make it up with some milk

Before you start this one, tip the marmalade into a bowl and give it a really good stir with a wooden spoon to loosen it up a bit. Then begin by sifting the flour, baking powder and salt into a bowl, lifting the sieve up high to give the flour a good airing. Next, in another bowl, whisk together the orange juice and zest, almonds, egg, milk and melted butter. Now return the dry ingredients to the sieve and sift them straight into the egg mixture. (This double sifting is crucial because we won't be doing much mixing.)

Now take a large metal spoon and fold the dry ingredients into the wet ones – the important thing is to do it quickly (i.e. in about 15 seconds). What you mustn't do is beat or stir, just fold it and ignore the uneven appearance of the mixture because it's precisely this that makes the muffins really light. Over-mixing is where people go wrong. Next, quickly fold in the marmalade (again no stirring).

Now divide the mixture between the muffin cases. Bake near the centre of the oven for 25 minutes until well-risen and golden brown. Remove the muffins from the oven, and transfer them straightaway to a wire rack to cool. Brush them with the extra marmalade. Store in an airtight tin.

BLUEBERRY & PECAN MUFFIN CAKE

Any of our muffin recipes can be adapted to any fruit, and
blueberries have always been popular, so in this recipe I decided, instead of making muffins,
I'd use the mixture to make a cake, which has turned out to be a real winner!

275g plain flour ◆ 1 level teaspoon ground cinnamon
1 level tablespoon baking powder ◆ ½ teaspoon salt
170ml milk ◆ 75g golden caster sugar ◆ 2 large eggs
110g block butter, melted and cooled slightly ◆ 275g blueberries

For the topping: 75g blueberries ◆ 1 heaped tablespoon demerara sugar
75g pecans, roughly chopped ◆ icing sugar for dusting

A 20cm loose-based cake tin, with non-stick liner (see page 13)
Pre-heat the oven to 190°C, gas mark 5

With muffins it's always a good idea to have everything weighed out and ready before you start

Begin by sifting the flour, cinnamon, baking powder and salt into a bowl, lifting
the sieve up high to give the flour a good airing. Now, in another bowl whisk together
the milk, sugar, eggs and melted butter. Then return the dry ingredients to the sieve and sift
them straight into the egg mixture. (This double sifting is crucial because we won't
be doing much mixing.)

Next take a large metal spoon and fold the dry ingredients quickly into the
wet ones – the key word here is quickly (i.e. in about 15 seconds). What you must
not do is beat or stir the mixture – just do the folding, and ignore the uneven appearance
of the mixture because it's precisely this that makes the muffins really light. Over-mixing
is where people go wrong. After that quickly fold in the blueberries (again no stirring).
Now spoon the mixture into the tin. Sprinkle the extra blueberries over,
followed by the demerara sugar and chopped pecans.

Place the cake near the centre of the oven and give it 1 hour, until it feels
springy in the centre. Let the cake cool in the tin for 30 minutes, then loosen it all
round with a palette knife. Place the cake tin on an upturned bowl or similar and gently
ease the sides down. Then loosen the base with a palette knife and transfer the cake to
a wire rack to finish cooling. Store in an airtight tin. Dust with a little
icing sugar just before serving.

SPICED APPLE MUFFINS

MAKES 6 LARGE MUFFINS

Apples, as I've said before, are good in cake recipes, adding fragrance as well as moisture. So they're perfect for muffins. In the autumn you could replace one of the apples with an equal weight of blackberries.

150g plain flour ◆ *1 level teaspoon ground cinnamon* ◆ *½ level teaspoon ground cloves*
1 level dessertspoon baking powder ◆ *¼ teaspoon salt* ◆ *1 large egg*
40g dark brown soft sugar ◆ *120ml milk* ◆ *50g block butter, melted and cooled slightly*
3 medium dessert apples, cored, then 2 grated and the other chopped into 1.5cm cubes

For the topping: *1 tablespoon demerara sugar, combined with*
½ level teaspoon cinnamon

A Silverwood muffin tray lined with 6 paper muffin cases (see page 16),
generously brushed with melted butter
Pre-heat the oven to 200C, gas mark 6

With muffins it's always a good idea to have everything weighed out and ready before you start

Begin by sifting the flour, spices, baking powder and salt into a bowl, lifting the sieve up high to give the flour a good airing. Now, in another bowl whisk together the egg, sugar, milk and melted butter, then return the dry ingredients to the sieve and sift them straight into the egg mixture. (This double sifting is crucial because we won't be doing much mixing.)

What you now need to do is take a large metal spoon and fold the dry ingredients quickly into the wet ones – the key word here is quickly (i.e. in about 15 seconds). What you mustn't do is beat or stir, just do the folding, and ignore the uneven appearance of the mixture because that's precisely what makes the muffins really light. Over-mixing is where people go wrong.

Next, quickly fold in the grated apple – again no stirring. Now divide the mixture between the muffin cases. Arrange the cubes of apple on top of each muffin, pressing them down slightly. Finally sprinkle with the sugar and cinnamon mixture. Bake near the centre of the oven for 25–30 minutes until well-risen and golden brown. Remove the muffins from the oven and transfer them straight away to a wire rack to cool. Store in an airtight tin or cake box.

RHUBARB & ORANGE MUFFINS

MAKES 6 LARGE MUFFINS

There were a few sceptics when, in my muffin madness, I suggested we try rhubarb.
But if you chop it small it does what other fruits do, and releases its juicy fragrance,
which permeates all through.

150g plain flour ◆ 1 level dessertspoon baking powder ◆ ¼ teaspoon salt
1 heaped tablespoon ground almonds ◆ zest and juice of 1 large orange
1 large egg ◆ 75g dark brown soft sugar ◆ 50g block butter, melted and slightly cooled
225g rhubarb, cut into 1.5cm cubes

For the topping: *1 heaped tablespoon demerara sugar*

A Silverwood muffin tray lined with 6 muffin paper cases (see page 16),
generously brushed with melted butter
Pre-heat the oven to 200°C, gas mark 6

With muffins it's always a good idea to have everything weighed out and ready before you start

Begin by sifting the flour, baking powder and salt into a bowl, lifting the sieve up high to
give the flour a good airing. Now, in another bowl, whisk together the almonds, orange juice and
zest, egg, sugar and melted butter. Return the dry ingredients to the sieve and sift them straight
into the egg mixture. (This double sifting is crucial because we won't be doing much mixing.)

What you now need to do is take a large metal spoon and fold the dry ingredients quickly
into the wet ones – the key word here is quickly (i.e. in about 15 seconds). What you mustn't do
is beat or stir, just fold, ignoring the uneven appearance of the mixture because that's precisely
what makes the muffins really light. Over-mixing is where people go wrong.

Next, quickly fold in the rhubarb – again no stirring. Now divide the mixture between
the muffin cases. Sprinkle on the demerara and bake near the centre of the oven for
25–30 minutes until well-risen and golden brown. Remove the muffins from the oven, and
transfer them straight away to a wire rack to cool. Store in an airtight tin or cake box.

DAMSON (OR PLUM) & CINNAMON MUFFINS

MAKES 6 LARGE MUFFINS

It's not easy to buy damsons, but it's worth searching in farm shops and markets at the end of August. However, if they're not forthcoming, you can still make these with chopped dark plums.

150g plain flour ◆ 1 level dessertspoon baking powder
1 level teaspoon ground cinnamon ◆ ¼ teaspoon salt ◆ 1 large egg
40g golden caster sugar ◆ 120ml milk ◆ 50g block butter, melted and cooled slightly
½ teaspoon vanilla extract ◆ 300g stoned damsons, halved (or plums, chopped)
25g flaked almonds

For the topping: 25g flaked almonds ◆ 1 heaped tablespoon demerara sugar, combined with
½ level teaspoon ground cinnamon

A Silverwood muffin tray lined with 6 paper muffin cases (see page 16),
generously brushed with melted butter
Pre-heat the oven to 200°C, gas mark 6

With muffins it's always a good idea to have everything weighed out and ready before you start

Begin by sifting the flour, baking powder, cinnamon and salt into a large bowl, lifting the sieve up high to give the flour a good airing. Now, in another bowl whisk together the egg, sugar, milk, melted butter and vanilla extract. Then return the dry ingredients to the sieve and sift them straight into the egg mixture. (This double sifting is crucial because we won't be doing much mixing.)

What you now need to do is take a large metal spoon and fold the dry ingredients quickly into the wet ones – the key word here is quickly (i.e. in about 15 seconds). What you mustn't do is beat or stir, just do the folding and ignore the uneven appearance of the mixture because it's precisely this that makes the muffins really light. Over-mixing is where people go wrong.

Next, quickly fold in the damsons and flaked almonds – again no stirring. Now divide the mixture between the muffin cases. Sprinkle on the topping and bake near the centre of the oven for 25–30 minutes until well-risen and golden brown. Remove the muffins from the oven, and transfer them straight away to a wire rack to cool. Store in an airtight tin.

FRESH GOOSEBERRY & ELDERFLOWER MUFFINS

MAKES 6 LARGE MUFFINS

What's good about changing seasons is looking forward to gooseberries, which only come once a year. They can of course be frozen but they're never quite as good, so once a year make these glorious and very special muffins.

150g plain flour ◆ 1 level dessertspoon baking powder ◆ ¼ teaspoon salt
1 large egg ◆ 40g golden caster sugar ◆ 2 tablespoons milk
75ml elderflower cordial ◆ 50g block butter, melted and cooled slightly
225g gooseberries, topped and tailed

For the topping: 18 extra (approx. 100g) gooseberries, topped and tailed
1 heaped tablespoon demerara sugar

A Silverwood muffin tray lined with 6 paper muffin cases (see page 16),
generously brushed with melted butter
Pre-heat the oven to 200°C, gas mark 6

With muffins it's always a good idea to have everything weighed out and ready before you start

Begin by sifting the flour, baking powder and salt into a bowl, lifting the sieve up high to give the flour a good airing. Now, in another bowl whisk together the egg, sugar, milk, elderflower cordial and melted butter. Then return the dry ingredients to the sieve and sift them straight into the egg mixture. (This double sifting is crucial because we won't be doing much mixing.)

What you now need to do is take a large metal spoon to fold the dry ingredients quickly into the wet ones – the key word here is quickly (i.e. in about 15 seconds). What you mustn't do is beat or stir, just do the folding and ignore the uneven appearance of the mixture because it's precisely this that makes the muffins really light. Over-mixing is where people go wrong.

Next, quickly fold in the gooseberries – again no stirring. Divide the mixture between the muffin cases. Lightly press 3 of the extra gooseberries into the top of each muffin. Sprinkle on the demerara sugar and bake just above the centre of the oven for 30 minutes until well-risen and golden brown. Remove the muffins from the oven, and transfer them straight away to a wire rack to cool. Store in an airtight tin.

SPICED CRANBERRY MUFFINS
with FROSTED CRANBERRIES

MAKES 6 LARGE MUFFINS

I just couldn't stop eating these when we tested them, so for me this is another reason to look forward to the Christmas season. They are great at any time, but would be especially good for a celebratory breakfast on Christmas morning.

150g plain flour ◆ 1 level teaspoon ground cinnamon ◆ 1 level teaspoon ground ginger
1 level dessertspoon baking powder ◆ ¼ teaspoon salt ◆ zest and juice of 1 large orange
1 large egg ◆ 75g golden caster sugar ◆ 1 tablespoon milk
50g block butter, melted and cooled slightly ◆ 225g cranberries

For the topping: 150g fondant icing sugar, sifted ◆ water

For the frosted cranberries: 18 cranberries ◆ 1 egg white, beaten
1 tablespoon white caster sugar

A Silverwood muffin tray lined with 6 paper muffin cases (see page 16),
generously brushed with melted butter
Pre-heat the oven to 200°C, gas mark 6

With muffins it's always a good idea to have everything weighed out and ready before you start

Begin by sifting the flour, cinnamon, ginger, baking powder and salt into a bowl, lifting the sieve up high to give the flour a good airing. Now, in another bowl whisk together the orange juice and zest, egg, sugar, milk and melted butter. Now return the dry ingredients to the sieve and sift them straight into the egg mixture. (This double sifting is crucial because we won't be doing much mixing.)

What you now need to do is take a large metal spoon to fold the dry ingredients quickly into the wet ones – the key word here is quickly (i.e. in about 15 seconds). What you mustn't do is beat or stir the mixture – just do the folding, and ignore the uneven appearance of the mixture because that's precisely what makes the muffins really light. Over-mixing is where people go wrong.

Next, quickly fold in the cranberries – again no stirring. Now divide the mixture between the muffin cases. Bake near the centre of the oven for 25–30 minutes until well-risen and golden brown. Remove the muffins from the oven and transfer to a wire cooling tray.

While they're cooling, make the frosted cranberries. All you need to do is dip each cranberry into beaten egg white and then roll it in caster sugar to give it a generous coating. Leave the berries spread out on baking parchment to become crisp.

Meanwhile place the icing sugar in a small bowl and gradually add water, a teaspoon at a time, to get a good spreading consistency. Then spread the icing over the cooled muffins using a small palette knife. Then top each one with 3 frosted cranberries.

Biscuits

GINGERNUTS

MAKES 16

Straight from the old book into the new, with not a hint of change.
Same crisp crunchiness, same snap as you break one in half, and same reminder of
how very much better they are homemade.

110g self-raising flour ◆ 1 slightly rounded teaspoon ground ginger
1 level teaspoon bicarbonate of soda ◆ 40g granulated sugar
50g block butter, at room temperature ◆ 50g (or 2 tablespoons) golden syrup

A large baking sheet, with a non-stick liner
Pre-heat the oven to 190°C, gas mark 5

Sift the flour, ground ginger and bicarbonate of soda together into a mixing bowl,
add the sugar, then lightly rub in the butter till crumbly. All you do now is simply add the syrup
and mix everything to a stiff paste. No liquid is needed because the syrup will be enough
to bring the mixture to the right consistency.

Now divide the mixture into quarters, as evenly sized as possible, then each
quarter into four, and roll the pieces into little balls. Next place them on the baking sheet,
leaving plenty of room between them because they spread out quite a bit. Then just flatten them
slightly (to about 1.5cm) and bake near the centre of the oven for 10–15 minutes by
which time they will have spread themselves out and will have a lovely cracked appearance.
Cool them on the baking tray for 10 minutes or so, then transfer them to a wire rack to finish
cooling and store in an airtight tin.

SEMOLINA SHORTBREADS

MAKES 12 WEDGES

This will always be the very best shortbread I've tasted. The secret of its success is the inclusion of semolina, which gives it that special texture. I will always be indebted to my friend John Tovey, who gave me the recipe.

175g plain flour ◆ 75g caster sugar ◆ 175g block butter, at room temperature
75g fine semolina ◆ a little extra caster sugar

One 20cm round loose-based sponge tin, lightly greased and base lined
Pre-heat the oven to 150°C, gas mark 2

Place all the ingredients in a mixing bowl and rub together until crumbly.
Bring together to a dough, using your hands.

Now transfer the dough to the prepared tin and press it out evenly, smoothing it out with the back of a tablespoon. Then prick it all over with a fork and, using the prongs of the fork, press quite firmly round the edges to make a patterned border.

Bake the shortbread near the centre of the oven for 1 to 1¼ hours until it is pale gold. Then allow the shortbread to cool in the tin for 10 minutes before cutting it into 12 wedges. Remove them to a wire rack to get completely cold, then sprinkle with sugar before storing in an airtight tin.

OAT & RAISIN COOKIES
MAKES ABOUT 24

No changes here on these almost classic biscuits, but now you could replace the raisins with dried sour cherries or dried cranberries to ring the changes.

75g block butter ◆ 1 large egg, beaten ◆ 175g dark brown soft sugar
200g medium oatmeal ◆ 110g wholemeal flour ◆ ½ teaspoon bicarbonate of soda
½ teaspoon salt ◆ 150g raisins

Two large baking sheets, well greased (or use liners)
Pre-heat the oven to 180°C, gas mark 4

Begin by heating the butter in a small saucepan very gently, then, when it's melted, remove it from the heat and leave it to cool a little before stirring in the beaten egg. Now measure the rest of the ingredients into a bowl, pour in the egg-and-butter mixture and stir to a stiff paste.

Form the paste into little balls, about the size of a walnut, and place them on greased baking sheets, giving them enough room to spread slightly during the baking, then press them down a little. Bake (one sheet at a time) near the centre of the oven for about 16–18 minutes, by which time the biscuits should feel fairly firm in the centre. Leave them to cool a little on the baking sheets then remove them to a cooling rack. Store in an airtight tin.

ALMOND TUILES

MAKES ABOUT 16

When you look at these you'll probably think 'I can't be bothered', but they are unbelievably easy to make and are the most elegant biscuits to serve with fruit fools and ice creams.

1 large egg white ◆ *50g golden caster sugar* ◆ *25g plain flour*
a few drops each of vanilla and almond extracts ◆ *25g block butter, melted*
40g flaked almonds

Two baking sheets, with non-stick liners
Pre-heat the oven to 220°C, gas mark 7

Place the egg white in a very clean bowl and whisk until stiff but not dry. Now beat in the sugar bit by bit and continue beating until the mixture forms soft peaks. When that happens, carefully fold in the rest of the ingredients except the almonds.

Next drop 4 rounded teaspoons of the mixture evenly spaced out on one of the lined trays, then using a small palette knife spread the mixture thinly and evenly into discs about 10cm across. Don't worry about a small hole here and there – it doesn't matter at all. Sprinkle with the flaked almonds, then bake the biscuits near the centre of the oven for 4–5 minutes or until they have turned a nice golden colour with a fine brown fringe.

While that's happening prepare the second tray so that you can exchange them. The cooked tuiles need to be quickly and carefully removed, one disc at a time, from the baking sheet, using a metal spatula. Curve each biscuit immediately over a rolling pin, and leave a few minutes until they are cool and crisp. Then remove them to a wire rack and cook the rest, continuing as above until all the mixture has been used up. As soon as the biscuits are cool, store straight away in an airtight tin to keep them crisp.

CHOCOLATE ORANGE BISCUITS

MAKES ABOUT 22

If you like chocolate and orange as a combination, then forget Jaffa Cakes.
These are in a completely different class.

125g spreadable butter ◆ 175g golden caster sugar
225g plain flour ◆ 2 level teaspoons baking powder ◆ 75g dark chocolate, chopped
zest of 2 oranges ◆ about 1 tablespoon orange juice
extra caster sugar for dusting

Two large baking sheets, greased or with non-stick liners
Pre-heat the oven to 180°C, gas mark 4

Start by beating the butter and sugar together with a wooden spoon until they're combined.
Then sift the flour and baking powder straight into the mixture. Add the rest of the ingredients,
and, still using the wooden spoon, work the mixture together until you get a fairly stiff paste.

Now flour a working surface and a rolling pin and roll the paste out to about 1cm thick.
Then, using a 5cm plain cutter, cut out the biscuits and place them on the baking sheets and bake
one sheet at a time near the centre of the oven. Bake them for about 20 minutes, or until the
biscuits are a nice golden colour.

Take them out of the oven and leave them to cool on the baking sheets for 5 minutes,
then transfer to a wire cooling tray, and finally sprinkle with a dusting of golden caster sugar.
Store in an airtight tin.

CHOCOLATE CHIP COOKIES

MAKES ABOUT 28

These have a history. In the first book someone – could have been me – failed to notice there were no chocolate chips included. We were informed by a lady who wrote a very nice letter, merely asking how much she should use. She won't need to write this time!

110g spreadable butter ◆ 150g light brown soft sugar ◆ 1 large egg, beaten
1 teaspoon vanilla extract ◆ 175g plain flour ◆ ½ teaspoon bicarbonate of soda
75g toasted chopped hazelnuts ◆ 100g dark, milk or white chocolate chips

Baking sheets, with non-stick liners
Pre-heat the oven to 180°C, gas mark 4

First put the butter and sugar together in a mixing bowl and beat with an electric hand whisk until light and fluffy. Then beat in the egg and the vanilla extract before folding in the remaining ingredients until thoroughly mixed. Now take slightly rounded dessertspoonfuls of the dough and arrange them (well spaced out) on baking sheets. Next flatten each one slightly, then bake them one sheet at a time on the shelf near the centre of the oven for about 15–16 minutes or until the biscuits have turned a dark golden colour and feel firm in the centre when lightly pressed.

As soon as the biscuits are baked, remove them from the baking sheets with the aid of a palette knife. Cool them on a wire rack and store in an airtight container.

FLORENTINES

MAKES ABOUT 20

If there was such a thing as a prize for the very best biscuit in the world, one bite
of a Florentine would tell you this was the winner. Absolutely top drawer and perfect if you
want to give a special homemade present at Christmas.

25g butter ◆ 75g golden caster sugar ◆ 10g plain flour (plus extra for dusting)
65ml double cream ◆ 50g whole almonds, cut into thin slivers
50g ready-flaked almonds ◆ 50g whole candied peel, chopped ◆ 25g glacé cherries, chopped
25g angelica, finely chopped (see page 224 for supplier)
175g dark chocolate (minimum 70% cocoa solids)

Two large baking sheets, with non-stick liners
Pre-heat the oven to 190°C, gas mark 5

Start by putting the butter together with the sugar and flour in a small,
heavy-based saucepan over a very low heat, and keep stirring until the mixture has melted. Now
gradually add the cream, stirring continuously to keep it smooth. Then add all the remaining
ingredients, except the chocolate. Stir thoroughly again, then remove the saucepan from
the heat and put the mixture on one side to cool.

You'll find it easier to bake one sheet of the Florentines at a time, so now place heaped
teaspoonfuls of the mixture onto one of the prepared baking sheets, spacing them about 2.5cm
apart (to allow the mixture room to expand while baking).

Flatten each spoonful with the back of the spoon, then bake on a high shelf for
about 10–12 minutes, or until golden. Then take them out of the oven and leave the biscuits
to harden on the baking sheet for 2–3 minutes, before quickly removing them to a wire
cooling tray to cool. Repeat with the second batch.

Next, melt the chocolate in a basin over a saucepan of barely simmering water,
making sure the base of the bowl doesn't touch the water. This will take about 5–10 minutes.
Place the cooled Florentines base-up on the wire rack and, using a teaspoon, coat the
underside of each Florentine with warm melted chocolate. Then, just before it sets, make a
patterned, wavy line on each one, using a fork. Now leave the Florentines to cool completely
before packing in alternating rows of fruit and chocolate side up in airtight tins.

GRASMERE GINGER SHORTBREADS

MAKES 12 WEDGES

I will always be grateful to the Hunter family in Cumbria who served these in their lakeside hotel, and who kindly gave me the recipe because I loved them so much.

110g plain flour ◆ 110g fine oatmeal ◆ 110g light brown soft sugar
1 heaped teaspoon ground ginger ◆ ¼ level teaspoon baking powder
150g block butter, well-chilled

A 20cm round loose-based sponge tin, greased and base lined
Pre-heat the oven to 180°C, gas mark 4

First combine the dry ingredients together in a bowl, making sure no little lumps remain. Then, holding it in a piece of foil, coarsely grate the chilled butter into the bowl, stopping now and then to fork the grated bits into the mixture so as to keep them separate. Finish off by using your hands to bind the butter into the dry ingredients until you have a uniform, sandy-textured mixture.

Now sprinkle this evenly into the prepared tin and press it down lightly over the surface. Bake the shortbread in the centre of the oven for about 45 minutes or until the mixture is just firm in the centre when lightly pressed. Now cool for 5 minutes then turn it out onto a wire rack and leave it to get quite cold. After that cut the shortbread into wedges and store in an airtight tin.

MACAROONS

MAKES 16

Light, almondy and chewy, most people love macaroons with their edible rice
paper bases. You may like to know that, for a change, the recipe works very well with ground
walnuts too (we call them Walleroons!).

90g ground almonds ◆ 10g icing sugar, sifted ◆ 1 level teaspoon ground rice
110g golden granulated sugar ◆ 1 large egg white ◆ a few drops almond extract
16 blanched almonds ◆ some golden caster sugar

A large baking sheet, lined with 2 sheets of rice paper (see page 224)
Pre-heat the oven to 150°C, gas mark 2

In a bowl mix the ground almonds together with the sifted icing sugar,
ground rice and granulated sugar. Now stir in the unbeaten egg white and a few drops
of almond extract and continue stirring until very thoroughly mixed. The mixture will be
sticky but what you now need to do is to divide it in the bowl into four and then divide
each quarter into four and roll each piece into a ball, using your hands.

Place the biscuits on the lined baking sheet, allowing room between each one for the
biscuits to expand during the cooking. Now dampen your fingers and press the biscuits
down a little into rounds. After that top each one with a blanched almond and finally
sprinkle on the caster sugar. Now bake the biscuits near the centre of the oven for
about 25–30 minutes, or until they are tinged a light golden brown.

Leave them to cool, then strip off the rice paper surrounding each biscuit.
Store them in an airtight tin as soon as they have cooled if you like to eat them crisp or,
if you prefer them a bit chewy, leave them overnight before storing in a tin.

CRYSTALLISED GINGER OAT BISCUITS

MAKES 12

These have always been personal favourites, and in this edition we have added chopped crystallised ginger and made them even better.

110g block butter ◆ 75g demerara sugar ◆ 1 dessertspoon golden syrup
110g self-raising flour ◆ 110g porridge oats ◆ 40g crystallised ginger, finely chopped
1 rounded teaspoon ground ginger ◆ pinch of salt

A large baking sheet (see page 13) with a non-stick liner
Pre-heat the oven to 170°C, gas mark 3

First, gently heat the butter, sugar and syrup together in a small saucepan until the sugar has dissolved. Meanwhile sift the flour into a bowl, then stir in the oats, the chopped and powdered ginger and salt. Now pour the melted mixture in and mix very thoroughly. Divide the mixture into four, and then divide each quarter into three and mould each piece into a little round with your hand.

Place them on the baking sheet, spacing them out well so that they have plenty of room to expand (which they will). Now press each one to flatten a little bit, then bake them near the centre of the oven for about 20–22 minutes, or until they've turned a lovely golden brown. Leave them on the baking sheet for 15 minutes, then transfer them to a wire cooling tray to finish cooling. Store them in an airtight tin to keep really crisp.

GARIBALDI BISCUITS

MAKES ABOUT 24

Still lovely after all these years. Still popular with children and with everyone else.

110g self-raising flour ◆ pinch of salt ◆ 25g spreadable butter
25g golden caster sugar ◆ 2 tablespoons milk ◆ 50g currants
a little egg white, lightly beaten ◆ a little granulated sugar

A large baking sheet, with a non-stick liner (see page 13)
Pre-heat the oven to 200°C, gas mark 6

Put the flour, salt and butter into a mixing bowl and rub to the fine crumb stage. Then add the sugar and after that enough milk to mix to a firm dough that will leave the bowl clean. After that transfer it to a lightly floured surface and roll it out to a rectangle 20cm by 30cm.

Now sprinkle the currants over half the surface and then fold the other half on top and roll everything again so you end up with a rectangle 20cm by 30cm. Then trim it neatly using a sharp long-bladed knife, so you end up with a shape about 18cm by 28cm. Cut this into 24 fingers approximately 3cm by 7cm. Now place the biscuits on the baking sheet, brush with a little egg white and sprinkle with granulated sugar. Bake near the centre of the oven for 12–15 minutes, then cool on a wire tray and store in an airtight tin.

PEANUT BUTTER BISCUITS

MAKES 28 BISCUITS

These, because they always love them, are good for children to make. But don't let that
stop you making them for grown-ups as well.

75g spreadable butter ◆ 110g chunky peanut butter ◆ 110g soft brown sugar
175g plain flour, plus a little extra ◆ 75g shelled unsalted peanuts
1 large egg, lightly beaten ◆ ¾ level teaspoon bicarbonate of soda
a little demerara sugar

Two large baking sheets, with non-stick liners (or greased)
Pre-heat the oven to 180°C, gas mark 4

First of all place all the ingredients (except the demerara sugar) in a bowl and mix
them together to form a stiffish dough. Now, because the mixture is sticky, flour your hands then
shape lumps of the mixture with your hands to form walnut-sized balls. Next tip a small heap of
demerara sugar onto a working surface and place a ball of mixture in the sugar. Flatten it
slightly, flip it over and place it (sugared side up) on the baking sheets.

The biscuits will spread, so allow some room for expansion. Bake them, one sheet at a
time, near the centre of the oven for 18 minutes, or until the biscuits feel firm when
tested with the fingertips.

Leave them to cool and harden slightly on the baking sheet before transferring
them to a wire cooling tray with the aid of a palette knife. Store them in an airtight tin.

ALMOND BISCOTTI

MAKES ABOUT 16

I think these twice-baked, very crisp biscuits are great for children to make and eat.
After that, the adults in true Italian fashion sit down with a glass of chilled Vin Santo, and
dip them into it before each bite.

110g plain flour ◆ ¾ level teaspoon baking powder ◆ pinch of salt
25g ground almonds ◆ 50g almonds, skins on ◆ 75g golden caster sugar
1 large egg, lightly beaten ◆ a few drops almond extract

A large baking sheet, with a non-stick liner (or greased)
Pre-heat the oven to 170°C, gas mark 3

First sift the flour, baking powder and salt into a large bowl, then add the ground
and whole almonds and sugar. Give it a good mix, then add the egg and the almond extract,
and mix it together first with a wooden spoon and then using your hands to bring the mixture
together to form a smooth dough.

Now place the dough on a lightly floured surface and, using your hands, roll it into
a log about 28cm long. Put it on the lined baking sheet and bake it near the centre of the oven for
30 minutes. After that, transfer it to a cooling tray and leave until completely cold.

Then reduce the oven temperature to 150°C, gas mark 2.

Now use a serrated knife to cut the biscotti into slightly diagonal slices about
1cm wide. Then place them back on the lined baking tray and bake for another 30 minutes until
pale gold and crisp. Transfer them to the cooling tray and when cold, store in
an airtight container.

WHOLE OAT CRUNCHIES

MAKES 12

These are the quickest and easiest biscuits I have ever made: they have a nice crunch and a toffee taste. A friend recently reminded me of these, so we tried them again and decided, yes, they absolutely had to be included.

50g jumbo oats ◆ 60g porridge oats ◆ 75g demerara sugar ◆ 110g block butter

A Silverwood oblong tin 20cm by 26cm, 4cm deep, base and sides lined with a non-stick liner (see page 13)
Pre-heat the oven to 190°C, gas mark 5

First weigh out the oats and sugar, place them in a bowl and mix them together as evenly as possible. Then gently melt the butter in a saucepan – only just melt it, be careful not to let it brown. Next pour the melted butter into the bowl with the oats and sugar and mix until everything is well and truly blended.

Now all you have to do is tip the mixture into the prepared tin and press it out evenly all over with the back of a tablespoon. Bake near the centre of the oven for 15–18 minutes or until a nice pale gold colour. Then remove the tin from the oven and cut the mixture into 12 portions while it is still warm. Leave in the tin until cold and crisp before storing the biscuits in an airtight tin.

GINGERBREAD MEN

MAKES ABOUT 15

This very well-behaved dough can put up with quite a bit of punishment, and is therefore ideal for children to play around with. You can buy proper cutters for making 'men' (see page 224) but in fact you (or your children) can pick any shaped cutter you like.

75g light brown soft sugar ◆ 2 tablespoons golden syrup ◆ 1 tablespoon black treacle
1 tablespoon water ◆ 1 teaspoon ground cinnamon ◆ 1 teaspoon ground ginger
pinch of cloves ◆ finely grated zest of ½ orange ◆ 95g block butter
½ teaspoon bicarbonate of soda ◆ 225g plain flour sifted, plus a little more (if needed)
1 tube of white writing icing (to decorate)

2 baking sheets, with non-stick liners

Put the sugar, syrup, treacle, water, spices and zest together in a large saucepan. Then bring them to boiling point, stirring all the time. Now remove the pan from the heat and stir in the butter (cut into lumps) and the bicarbonate of soda.

Next stir in the flour gradually until you have a smooth manageable dough – add a little more flour if you think it needs it. Now leave the dough covered in a cool place to become firm (approximately 30 minutes). Pre-heat the oven to 180°C, gas mark 4.

Now roll the dough out to 3mm thick on a lightly floured surface and cut out the gingerbread men. Arrange them on the baking sheets and bake near the centre of the oven, one sheet at a time, for 10–15 minutes until the biscuits feel firm when lightly pressed with a fingertip. Leave them to cool on the baking sheet for a few minutes before transferring them to a wire cooling rack.

To decorate, use the icing to write names or make faces. Store in an airtight container.

Chocolate Cakes

CHOCOLATE FRUIT &
NUT REFRIGERATOR CAKE

This is obviously perfect for children to make because there's no cooking involved.
But the grown-up version could include other combinations of fruits and nuts (prunes,
crystallised ginger, dried sour cherries, etc).

150g dark chocolate (minimum 70% cocoa solids), broken into pieces,
or 150g milk chocolate (30% cocoa solids) broken into pieces
25g block butter ◆ 100ml double cream
75g blanched hazelnuts, roasted (see page 42) and cooled
75g raisins ◆ 150g very crisp sweet biscuits, roughly chopped
(we like biscotti, ginger nuts or any oat biscuits)
cocoa powder (to dust)

An 18cm by 4cm loose-based sponge tin, with a non-stick liner (see page 13)

First place the chocolate in a bowl with the butter and fit the bowl over a pan
containing 5cm of barely simmering water, making sure the bowl doesn't touch the water.
Then turn the heat to its lowest setting and allow the chocolate to melt (which should take
about 5–10 minutes). After that remove the bowl from the pan and give it all a good stir
till it's smooth and glossy.

Now allow it to cool for about 3 minutes. While it's cooling, whip the cream
to the floppy stage, then fold it into the cooled chocolate mixture. Follow this with the
nuts, fruit and chopped biscuits, giving it all a really good mix. Finally spoon it into
the cake tin as evenly as possible and level it off with the back of a spoon.

Cover the tin with clingfilm and chill for a minimum of 4 hours. Just before serving, dust
the surface with a little cocoa powder then remove the cake from the tin and cut into wedges.
It's great as a dessert with some crème fraiche or pouring cream; or cut into small cubes for
after dinner with coffee. Store in a polythene box in the fridge.

SACHERTORTE

This is a perennial favourite, named after the famous Viennese hotel, where
you can still buy it in boxes and bring it home. It's dark, very chocolatey and sophisticated,
and for a special occasion or a birthday, it's nice to decorate it with sugared rose petals
(for a recipe see page 202).

175g dark chocolate (minimum 70% cocoa solids) ◆ 110g plain flour
1 level teaspoon baking powder ◆ 110g spreadable butter ◆ 110g golden caster sugar
a few drops almond extract ◆ 4 large egg yolks, beaten ◆ 5 large egg whites

For the icing: 175g dark chocolate (minimum 70% cocoa solids)
150ml double cream ◆ 1 level dessertspoon glycerine ◆ 1 level dessertspoon apricot jam

A 20cm round loose-based cake tin, greased, with a non-stick base liner (see page 13)
Pre-heat the oven to 150°C, gas mark 2

Place the broken-up chocolate in a bowl over a pan containing 5cm of
barely simmering water, without the bowl touching the water. When it's melted
(5–10 minutes) take it off the heat.

While that's happening, sift the flour and baking powder into a roomy
mixing bowl, lifting the sieve quite high to give the flour a good airing as it goes down.
Then add the butter, sugar, almond extract and beaten egg yolks, and, using an electric hand
whisk, combine them for about 1 minute until you have a smooth creamy consistency. After
that beat the chocolate into the creamed mixture. Now, using a clean dry whisk and a
large bowl, whisk the egg whites to soft peaks and then carefully and gradually fold
them into the mixture bit by bit, using a metal spoon.

Pour the mixture into the prepared cake tin, level the top with the back of a tablespoon
and bake it near the centre of the oven for about 40–45 minutes, or until firm, well-risen and
springy in the centre. When it's cooked, allow the cake to cool in the tin for 10 minutes before
turning it out onto a cooling rack (see page 12) and leaving it to get quite cold.

To make the icing: melt the chocolate (as above), then remove it from the heat.
Stir in the cream and the glycerine till thoroughly blended. Now warm the apricot jam
and brush the cake all over with it. Finally pour the icing over the whole cake, using a palette
knife to cover the top and sides completely. Then leave it to set (which will take 2–3 hours).
If you make it in advance you can store it in the fridge once the icing has set. Serve cut in
wedges – in Vienna they always serve it with a generous amount of whipped cream.

CHOCOLATE BEER CAKE

The beer – dark stout (Guinness, Murphy's or similar) – gives this cake an extra dimension, and the icing is so good it can be used on other chocolate cakes.

175g self-raising flour ◆ ¼ level teaspoon baking powder
1 level teaspoon bicarbonate of soda ◆ 275g dark brown soft sugar ◆ 110g spreadable butter
2 large eggs, beaten ◆ 50g cocoa powder, sifted ◆ 200ml sweet stout

For the icing: 110g dark chocolate (minimum 70% cocoa solids), broken up
2 tablespoons sweet stout ◆ 50g spreadable butter ◆ 110g icing sugar, sifted
25g walnut pieces, finely chopped

To decorate: 8 walnut halves

Two 20cm loose-based round sponge tins, greased with base liners (see page 13),
plus two wire cooling trays
Pre-heat the oven to 180°C, gas mark 4

All you do is sift the flour, baking powder and bicarbonate of soda into a roomy mixing bowl, lifting the sieve quite high to give the flour a good airing as it goes down. Then simply add all the other ingredients, except the stout. Now, using an electric hand whisk, combine them for about one minute until you have a smooth creamy consistency. Finally stir in the stout, a little at a time, until it's all incorporated.

Next divide the mixture between the two prepared tins and bake near the centre of the oven for about 30–35 minutes. They are cooked when you press lightly with your little finger and the centre springs back.

Then remove them from the oven and after about 30 seconds loosen the edges by sliding a palette knife all round then turn them out onto a wire cooling tray. Carefully peel back the lining by gently pulling it back. Now lightly place the other cooling tray on top and just flip them over so that the tops are facing upwards (this is to prevent them sticking to the cooling tray).

To make the icing: melt the broken chocolate with the stout in a bowl set over a pan containing 5cm of barely simmering water, without the bowl touching the water. When it's melted (5–10 minutes) take it off the heat. Beat in the butter and leave it to cool a little before beating in the icing sugar with an electric hand whisk. Now transfer a third of the icing to a separate bowl and stir the chopped walnuts into that.

After the icings have cooled to a spreadable consistency, sandwich the cake with the walnut icing, then spread the remaining two thirds of the icing on the top of the cake, using a palette knife. Finally decorate with a circle of walnut halves. Leave the icing to set completely before storing in an airtight tin.

GRATED CHOCOLATE & ALMOND CAKE

I feel somewhat constrained when trying endlessly to explain the merits of cakes to people who have not tried them, but there is only one word for this one. Magnificent. It's very special – the almonds give it a very moist texture and the little flecks of chocolate give a different sort of chocolate experience.

110g spreadable butter ◆ 175g golden caster sugar ◆ 4 large eggs, separated
6 tablespoons milk ◆ 175g self-raising flour, sifted ◆ 110g ground almonds
110g grated dark chocolate (minimum 70% cocoa solids), chilled

To decorate: 175g dark chocolate (minimum 70% cocoa solids), broken up
1 rounded tablespoon crème fraiche

A 20cm round loose-based cake tin, greased and base lined (see page 13)
Pre-heat the oven to 220°C, gas mark 7

Place the butter, sugar, egg yolks, milk, flour and ground almonds in a large mixing bowl, then whisk for about 1–2 minutes until smooth. Now fold in the grated chocolate.

Next, in a separate dry, clean bowl whisk the egg whites till they reach the soft peak stage, and then fold half of them into the rest of the mixture gently and carefully so as not to lose all the air you have whisked in. Repeat with the other half. Next spoon the mixture into the prepared tin, level it off with the back of a tablespoon, place it near the centre of the oven, reduce the heat to 170°C, gas mark 3 and bake for 1 hour or until the centre is springy when lightly touched.

Allow the cake to stand in the tin for 5 minutes before sliding a palette knife round the edge. Now ease it out of the tin by placing it on an upturned bowl (see page 12), then using the palette knife slide it off the base onto a wire rack to cool.

Now put the broken-up chocolate in a bowl over a pan containing 5cm of barely simmering water, without the bowl touching the water. When it's melted (5–10 minutes) take it off the heat and stir in the crème fraiche. Allow it to cool and thicken slightly, then split the cake in half. I have found the best way to do this is to sit down with the cake on a board and hold it steady with one hand and then with a serrated knife use a gentle sawing movement to slice horizontally through the cake. Use half the chocolate to sandwich it together, and the other half to spread over the top, making patterns with a knife. Store in an airtight tin till needed.

MOIST CHOCOLATE & RUM SQUARES

MAKES 12

If there is an ultimate chocolate cake this one could be high on the list of contenders. No flour, just chocolate, ground almonds and whipped egg whites which make it so light and airy, and extremely moist. It doesn't have to be cut into squares, you could serve it as a cake with candles or Easter eggs on top. Either way it is one of the best chocolate cakes ever.

150g spreadable butter ◆ 150g golden caster sugar ◆ 5 large eggs, separated
150g ground almonds ◆ 150g grated dark chocolate (minimum 70% cocoa solids), chilled

For the icing: 110g dark chocolate (minimum 70% cocoa solids), broken up
1 tablespoon double cream or crème fraiche ◆ 2 tablespoons rum

A Silverwood oblong tin 20cm by 26cm, 4cm deep, base and sides lined
with non-stick liner (see page 13)

Pre-heat the oven to 170°C, gas mark 3

First place the butter, sugar and egg yolks in a bowl and whisk them for about a minute until thoroughly blended. Then fold in the almonds and grated chocolate. Now, with a clean dry whisk, whisk the egg whites to the soft peak stage – not too stiff – and then carefully fold half into the chocolate mixture, followed by the other half.

Spread the mixture in the prepared tin, levelling it with the back of a tablespoon, and bake near the centre of the oven for about 55 minutes to 1 hour or until it feels springy in the centre. Leave the cake to cool in the tin, and then lift the cake out using the liner. Place it on a board, then holding the liner at one end, use a palette knife to slide the cake directly onto the board.

Now put the broken-up chocolate in a bowl over a pan of 5cm barely simmering water, without the bowl touching the water. When it's melted (5–10 minutes), take it off the heat and stir in the cream and 1 tablespoon of rum. Then let the icing cool and thicken a bit. Sprinkle the surface of the cake with the other tablespoon of rum, and spread with the cooled chocolate icing, using a palette knife. Leave the icing to set before cutting it into squares. Then store in an airtight tin.

BRAZIL NUT BROWNIES

Brownies need introducing to those who have not yet made them. Yes, they are cakes but not in the conventional sense. They are supposed to be moist and squashy, and although they won't look as if they are cooked, they are. Don't think you may have failed, just bite into one and you'll never look back.

125g dark chocolate (minimum 70% cocoa solids), broken up ◆ 175g block butter
3 large eggs ◆ 275g golden caster sugar ◆ 75g plain flour ◆ 1 level teaspoon baking powder
¼ teaspoon salt ◆ 150g Brazil nuts, toasted (see page 42) and roughly chopped, or any
other nuts, or a mixture

A Silverwood oblong tin 20cm by 26cm, 4cm deep, greased and lined (see page 13)

Pre-heat the oven to 180°C, gas mark 4

First put the broken-up chocolate and butter in a bowl over a pan containing 5cm of barely simmering water, without the bowl touching the water. When it has melted (5–10 minutes) take it off the heat. Next whisk the eggs and sugar lightly together – but don't overdo this. Stir the egg mixture and all the other ingredients into the chocolate.

Then pour the mixture into the tin and bake near the centre of the oven for 30 minutes until springy in the middle. Leave the cake in the tin to go completely cold before dividing into roughly twelve squares and store in an airtight tin.

CHOCOLATE MARBLED ENERGY BARS

MAKES 15

I made these on TV with Dawn French for Comic Relief. After that, school children were making them all over the country to raise money – and they were very popular. We also like them without the chocolate topping.

110g chopped toasted pecan nuts (see page 42) ◆ *110g ready-to-eat dried apricots, chopped small*
75g raisins ◆ *150g porridge oats* ◆ *25g Rice Krispies* ◆ *25g Bran Flakes, lightly crushed*
1 rounded teaspoon molasses syrup ◆ *150ml whole condensed milk*

For the topping: 150g dark chocolate (minimum 70% cocoa solids), broken into small pieces
150g luxury Belgian white chocolate, broken into small pieces

A Silverwood oblong tin 20cm by 26cm, 4cm deep, with a liner (see page 13)
Pre-heat the oven to 180°C, gas mark 4

First place the nuts, apricots, raisins and cereals in a bowl, then put the molasses syrup and condensed milk in a small saucepan and heat them gently until they are warmed through and blended together. Now pour this mixture into the bowl and mix well with a wooden spoon till everything is thoroughly blended, and after that tip it into the baking tin. Press it down evenly all over and bake in the centre of the oven for about 25 minutes until it's golden brown. Then remove it from the oven and let it get quite cold.

Meanwhile melt the dark and white chocolate separately in bowls set over small pans containing about 5cm of barely simmering water – the bowls shouldn't touch the water. They should take 5–10 minutes to melt.

Now loosen the edges of the cake and turn it out onto a board, then turn it the other way up so the smoother surface is underneath. Using a tablespoon, put spoonfuls of the plain chocolate all over the top of the cereal cake, leaving space in between. Then do the same with the white chocolate, filling all the gaps in between. Next take a small palette knife and, using a zig-zag motion, swirl the two chocolates together to give a marbled effect. Then lift the board and give it a gentle tap on the work surface to create a smooth finish.

Now you need to chill the mixture in the fridge for about one hour. Then, using a sharp knife, cut it into 15 squares. Store in an airtight tin until needed.

Celebration Cakes

THE ULTIMATE CARROT CAKE

Well, it has to be said. There have been many versions over the years, but this is the ultimate and it's great for a birthday or any other celebration. At the football club we make them into little cakes, and half the mixture makes six large or twelve small cup cakes.

*175g dark brown soft sugar ◆ 2 large eggs ◆ 150ml sunflower oil
200g wholemeal self-raising flour ◆ 3 level teaspoons mixed spice
1 level teaspoon bicarbonate of soda ◆ 200g carrots, peeled and coarsely grated
grated zest of 1 orange ◆ 110g sultanas ◆ 50g desiccated coconut
50g toasted pecan nuts (see page 42), chopped*

*For the cinnamon icing: 2 x 250g tubs mascarpone ◆ 1 heaped teaspoon ground cinnamon
2 tablespoons milk (or orange juice) ◆ 1 rounded tablespoon golden caster sugar
50g chopped toasted pecan nuts (to finish)*

*For the syrup glaze: 75g dark brown soft sugar ◆ juice of 1 small orange
1 tablespoon lemon juice*

*Two 20cm by 4cm sponge tins, bases lined (see page 13)
Pre-heat the oven to 170°C, gas mark 3*

First place the sugar, eggs and oil in a bowl and whisk them together with an electric hand whisk for 2–3 minutes until the sugar has dissolved. Next sift the flour, spice and bicarbonate of soda into the bowl – the little bits of bran left in the sieve can be tipped in at the end. Now fold all this in gently. After that, add the rest of the cake ingredients. Then divide the mixture evenly between the prepared tins and level them off with the back of a tablespoon. Bake the cakes near the centre of the oven for 30 minutes until they are springy and firm in the centre.

While the cakes are cooking make the icing by simply whisking the mascarpone, cinnamon, milk (or orange juice) and sugar in a bowl till smooth and fluffy. Then cover the bowl and chill until needed.

For the syrup glaze, whisk together the sugar and fruit juices in another bowl, and as soon as the cakes come out of the oven, first stab them all over with a skewer and then spoon the syrup evenly over the hot cakes. After that they need to cool in their tins in order to soak up all of the syrup.

As soon as they are completely cold remove them from the tins (see page 12). Place one of the cakes on a serving plate, spread one third of the icing all over, then place the other cake on top and finally cover the top and sides with the remaining mixture. If you are not going to serve it straight away, cover and chill until needed. But don't forget to decorate with the nuts just before serving.

SQUIDGY CHOCOLATE CAKE

In the late '70s this cake went down a storm, and still people tell me they always have it on their birthday! Because it is not made with flour it's incredibly light and soufflé-like. Then it's filled and topped with chocolate mousse, whipped cream and shards of chocolate. It's also great at Easter, decorated with sugar-coated chocolate eggs.

225g dark chocolate (minimum 70% cocoa solids) ◆ *100ml warm water* ◆ *8 large eggs*
110g golden caster sugar ◆ *50g cocoa powder* ◆ *425ml double cream*

To decorate: 100g dark chocolate (minimum 70% cocoa solids)

A Silverwood Swiss Roll tin 20cm by 30cm, greased and lined with a single sheet of baking parchment or liner (see page 13), so that it comes up 2.5cm above the edge of the rim
Pre-heat the oven to 180°C, gas mark 4

Start off by making the chocolate filling. Put the broken-up chocolate and water in a bowl over a pan containing 5cm of barely simmering water, without the bowl touching the water. When it has melted (5–10 minutes), take it off the heat and beat with a wooden spoon until smooth.

Now separate two of the eggs and beat the yolks, first on their own, then into the warm chocolate mixture. Let it cool a bit. Now, with an absolutely clean whisk, whisk the egg whites till stiff and fold them into the chocolate mixture. Cover the bowl and chill in the refrigerator for 30–45 minutes. Then remove from the refrigerator, or it will get too stiff.

Now for the cake. First separate the remaining six large eggs, putting the whites into a large mixing bowl and the yolks into another. Whisk the yolks with an electric hand whisk until they begin to thicken. Then add the caster sugar and continue whisking until the mixture feels thick – but don't overdo it, it shouldn't be starting to turn pale. Now quickly whisk in the cocoa powder.

Next, using a clean dry whisk, beat the egg whites till they are stiff and form little peaks. At this point, take a metal spoon and carefully fold them into the egg yolk mixture, gently and thoroughly and making sure you get right down to the bottom of the bowl with the spoon.

Pour the mixture into the prepared tin, spread it evenly with the back of a tablespoon and bake on a highish shelf in the oven for about 20–25 minutes until risen and puffy like a soufflé (it won't look as if it's cooked – but it will be). Remove it from the oven and don't be alarmed as it starts to sink because it's supposed to – when it is cool, it will look crinkly on the surface.

To turn the cake out, place a piece of baking parchment on a flat surface. Then, before you turn it out, gently loosen the sides of the cake away from the liner, and turn it out onto the paper. Lift the tin away from the cake and carefully peel off the lining. Now cut the cake evenly in half (not lengthways – i.e. you need to end up with two squarish oblongs). Now to prepare the topping and filling: first place the chocolate on a board and, with a large sharp knife, cut it into thin shards starting at one end and working all along it. Next whip the cream until quite thick. Now place one half of the cake on a serving plate, then, using a palette knife, spread half the chocolate mixture over one half of the cake, and about a quarter of the cream over the chocolate and sprinkle it with half of the chopped chocolate. Place the other half of the cake on top, forming a sandwich (a pan slice will assist you here). Now spread the rest of the chocolate mixture on top, and then cover the whole cake (sides as well) with whipped cream.

Sprinkle the remaining chopped chocolate all over the top of the cake. Keep it covered loosely with foil or clingfilm in the fridge until you are ready to serve. We think this is best eaten on the same day but it will keep for a couple of days in the fridge.

CLASSIC CHRISTMAS CAKE

This is my original Christmas cake from the first book – a combination of my grandmother's, my mother's and a few tweaks from me.

For the pre-soaking: ◆ *450g currants* ◆ *175g sultanas* ◆ *175g raisins*
50g chopped glacé cherries ◆ *50g mixed chopped candied peel* ◆ *100ml brandy*

For the cake: 225g plain flour ◆ *½ teaspoon salt* ◆ *¼ level teaspoon nutmeg, freshly grated*
½ level teaspoon ground mixed spice ◆ *225g dark brown soft sugar*
4 large eggs ◆ *1 dessertspoon black treacle* ◆ *225g spreadable butter*
50g chopped almonds (skin on) ◆ *zest of 1 lemon and 1 orange*

Armagnac or brandy, to 'feed' the cake
100g whole blanched almonds (only if you don't intend to ice the cake)
A 20cm round loose-based cake tin, greased, with base and side lined (see page 13),
plus some baking parchment. Tie a double band of brown paper around the outside
of the tin for extra protection

You should get the pre-soaking ingredients ready the night before you make the cake. Put all the fruits in a bowl and mix them with the brandy, cover with a cloth and leave them to soak for a minimum of 12 hours.

When you're ready to cook the cake, pre-heat the oven to 140 °C, gas mark 1. Now all you do is sift the flour, salt and spices into a very large roomy mixing bowl then add the sugar, eggs, treacle (warm it a little first to make it easier) and butter and beat with an electric hand whisk until everything is smooth and fluffy. Now gradually fold in the pre-soaked fruit mixture, chopped nuts and finally the grated lemon and orange zests.

Next, using a large kitchen spoon, transfer the cake mixture into the prepared tin, spread it out evenly with the back of the spoon and, if you don't intend to decorate the cake with marzipan and icing, lightly drop the blanched almonds in circles over the surface.

Finally take a double square of baking parchment with a 50p-sized hole in the centre (for extra protection during the cooking) and place this *not* on top of the mixture itself but on the rim of the brown paper. Bake the cake on the lowest shelf of the oven for 4 hours until it feels springy in the centre when lightly touched. Sometimes it can take 30–45 minutes longer than this, but in any case don't look at it for 4 hours.

Cool the cake for 30 minutes in the tin, then remove it to a wire rack to finish cooling. When it's cold, 'feed' it by making small holes in the top and bottom with a cocktail stick and spooning in a couple of tablespoons of Armagnac or brandy, then wrap it in parchment-lined foil (see page 225) and store in an airtight tin. You can now 'feed' it at odd intervals until you need to ice or eat it.

Note: for icing instructions, see pages 200–201, 203, 204.

LAST-MINUTE CHRISTMAS MINCEMEAT CAKE

Self-explanatory, I think. You didn't have time, you don't want the factory version, so this one made simply with a jar of mincemeat will make a really speedy but excellent alternative.

For the pre-soaking: *150ml brandy ◆ 1 x 400g (approximately) jar luxury mincemeat 110g no-soak prunes, roughly chopped ◆ 50g glacé cherries, quartered 175g dried mixed fruit ◆ 50g whole candied peel, finely chopped*

For the cake: *225g self-raising flour, sifted ◆ 3 level teaspoons baking powder ¼ teaspoon salt ◆ 1½ level teaspoons mixed spice ◆ 150g spreadable butter 150g dark muscovado sugar ◆ 3 large eggs 50g Brazil nuts, roughly chopped ◆ 50g mixed chopped nuts zest of 1 small orange and 1 small lemon ◆ approximately 18 walnut halves, 18 pecan halves, 20 whole Brazils (or any other mixture you like)*

For the glaze: *1 heaped tablespoon sieved apricot jam ◆ 1 tablespoon brandy*

A 20cm round loose-based cake tin, greased with base and side lined (see page 13), plus some baking parchment

Even though this is last-minute, it's best to pre-soak the fruits if you can. So just measure out the brandy, mincemeat and fruits into a bowl, give them a good stir, then cover with a cloth and leave somewhere cool overnight or for a minimum of 4 hours.

When you are ready to make the cake, pre-heat the oven to 170 °C, gas mark 3. Now all you do is sift the flour, baking powder, salt and mixed spice into a very large roomy mixing bowl, then add the butter, sugar and eggs and beat with an electric hand whisk until everything is smooth and fluffy. Now gradually fold in the pre-soaked fruit mixture, chopped nuts and finally the grated lemon and orange zests. Now take a large spoon and spoon it into the prepared tin, levelling the top with the back of the spoon, then arrange the whole nuts in circles or rows on the surface.

Finally, take a double square of baking parchment with a 50p-sized hole in the centre (which gives it extra protection during the cooking) and place this *not* on the top of the mixture itself but on the rim of the liner. Bake the cake on the centre shelf of the oven for 2 hours or until the centre springs back when lightly touched. Cool the cake in the tin for 30 minutes, then remove it to a wire cooling tray to continue cooling.

While that's happening, heat the apricot jam and brandy together and brush the nuts with this mixture to make them shiny and glossy. Store the cake in an airtight tin or in parchment-lined foil (see page 225) and it will keep beautifully.

CREOLE CHRISTMAS CAKE

If there were a Delia's Christmas cake poll this would now be a clear leader. Originally from the Caribbean, it does involve quite a lot of booze and a week's pre-soaking; but one thing's for sure, you'll want to make it again and again so all those bottles will be awaiting you next year.

For the pre-soaking: 3 tablespoons rum ◆ 3 tablespoons brandy ◆ 3 tablespoons cherry brandy
3 tablespoons port ◆ 3 tablespoons water ◆ 1½ teaspoons Angostura bitters
½ level teaspoon ground cinnamon ◆ ½ level teaspoon nutmeg, freshly grated
½ level teaspoon ground cloves ◆ ½ teaspoon salt ◆ 1½ teaspoons pure vanilla extract
1 level tablespoon molasses sugar ◆ 450g raisins ◆ 225g currants ◆ 110g no-soak prunes, chopped
50g glacé cherries, chopped ◆ 110g whole candied peel, finely chopped ◆ 50g mixed chopped nuts

For the cake: 250g self-raising flour ◆ 250g demerara sugar
250g spreadable butter ◆ 5 large eggs

A 20cm round loose-based cake tin, greased with base and side lined (see page 13),
plus some baking parchment

About 7 days before you want to make the cake, measure out all the pre-soaking ingredients into a large saucepan, ticking them off as you add them as it's so easy to leave something out! Now place the mixture over a medium heat and bring it up to simmering point, giving everything a good stir. Then turn the heat down to very low and let everything simmer without covering for about 15 minutes.

After that remove the pan from the heat and let everything get completely cold. Then transfer the mixture to an airtight plastic container and leave it in the fridge for a week, giving it a shake or a stir from time to time.

When you want to bake the cake, pre-heat the oven to 140°C, gas mark 1. Then sift the flour into a large bowl, add the sugar, butter and eggs and, using an electric hand whisk (or a wooden spoon), beat until everything is thoroughly blended. After that gradually fold in the soaked mixture until it's all evenly distributed. Now transfer the mixture to the prepared tin, and level with a back of a spoon.

Place the cake near the centre of the oven and bake it for 3 hours, then cover with a double thickness of baking parchment, resting it on top of the liner, and bake it for another hour, until the centre feels springy.

Allow the cake to cool in the tin for 45 minutes, then transfer it to a wire cooling tray to cool. When it's absolutely cold, wrap it in parchment-lined foil (see page 225) and store in an airtight tin or polythene box.

Note: if you would like to make a smaller Creole cake, use half the mixture with 3 medium eggs and bake in an 18cm round tin for 2 hours and 50 minutes, covering with the parchment after the first 2 hours. For icing instructions, see pages 200–201, 203, 204.

LIGHT CHRISTMAS CAKE

Unlike the dark, traditional cakes this one is light in colour but filled with jewelled crystallised fruits. It would be a perfect choice for someone who wants something completely different. For crystallised fruit stockists see page 224.

110g walnuts ◆ 110g glacé pineapple ◆ 110g ready-to-eat dried apricots
175g glacé cherries (red, green & yellow), rinsed and dried ◆ 225g sultanas
110g candied peel ◆ 50g angelica (see page 224 for suppliers) ◆ 50g crystallised ginger
225g plain flour, sifted ◆ 225g golden caster sugar
50g ground almonds ◆ ¼ teaspoon salt
225g spreadable butter ◆ 4 large eggs ◆ 3 tablespoons brandy
zests of 1 orange and 1 lemon ◆ 1 tablespoon lemon juice

A 20cm loose-based round cake tin, greased with base and side lined (see page 13), plus some baking parchment and brown paper

Pre-heat the oven to 170°C, gas mark 3

To begin this cake you need to do quite a bit of chopping. Start with the walnuts, which should be fairly finely chopped. Then the pineapple, apricots and cherries need to be chopped roughly the same size as the sultanas. The candied peel, angelica and crystallised ginger need to be chopped smaller.

Now take a large roomy bowl, sift in the flour, then add the caster sugar, ground almonds, salt, butter, eggs and brandy and, using an electric hand whisk, whisk everything thoroughly for about a minute until smooth and creamy. Now fold in all the fruits, the nuts, grated zests and the lemon juice.

Next, using a large spoon, transfer the cake mixture to the tin and level off the top with the back of the spoon. Now tie a band of brown paper around the tin to give extra protection, and place the tin in the oven so the top of it is more or less in the centre. Bake the cake for one hour, then place a double sheet of baking parchment over the top so it sits on the liner and turn the heat down to 150°C, gas mark 2 for a further 2 hours.

When it's cooked it will be springy in the centre when you press lightly with your little finger. You can leave this cake in the tin till it's absolutely cold, then remove from the tin (see page 12), peel off the liners and wrap it in parchment-lined foil (see page 225) to store in an airtight tin.

Note: for decorations see page 205.

EASTER SIMNEL CAKE

What is Simnel cake? A rich fruit cake which includes lumps of marzipan stirred into the mixture that melts and combines with all the other flavours during cooking. It is then finished off with more marzipan. As it's now popular at Easter, sugared primroses make a good decoration (for a recipe see page 202). For stockists see page 224.

225g natural marzipan ◆ 225g plain flour ◆ 1 level teaspoon baking powder
1 level teaspoon mixed spice ◆ 175g spreadable butter ◆ 175g golden caster sugar
3 large eggs ◆ 3 tablespoons milk ◆ 175g currants ◆ 225g sultanas
50g glacé cherries, rinsed, dried, and cut into quarters
50g unblanched almonds, roasted and chopped (see page 42)
50g chopped candied peel ◆ zest of 1 orange and 1 lemon

For the topping: 300g natural marzipan ◆ 1 rounded dessertspoon apricot jam
sugared yellow primroses

A 20cm round loose-based cake tin, greased with base and side lined (see page 13),
plus some baking parchment
Pre-heat the oven to 150°C, gas mark 2

First of all cut the marzipan into 1cm cubes and then toss them in 2 level tablespoons of flour (taken from the measured amount above). Now sift the remaining flour, the baking powder and spice into a roomy mixing bowl, holding the sieve quite high to give the flour a good airing as it goes down, then add the butter, caster sugar and eggs. Now, using an electric hand whisk, mix to a smooth, creamy consistency for about 1 minute. Then whisk in the milk.

Take a metal spoon and gently fold in the fruit, nuts, candied peel and grated orange and lemon zests followed by the marzipan cubes. Now spoon the mixture into the prepared tin and level it out with the back of the spoon. Finally, take a double square of baking parchment with a 50p-sized hole in the centre (for extra protection during cooking) and place this *not* on the top of the mixture itself but on the rim of the liner. Bake the cake near the centre of the oven for about 2 hours 40 minutes – or until the centre is firm and springy.

Leave the cake in the tin to cool for 15 minutes before turning it out onto a wire rack. Roll out the marzipan to a round approximately 22cm in diameter. Brush the top of the cooled cake with apricot jam, top with the round of marzipan, and scallop the edges using your thumb and forefinger.

Finally, to toast the marzipan: cut out a circle of foil to cover the top of the cake inside the scalloped edge and place the cake under a pre-heated grill so the marzipan is 10cm from the heat source for 1½–2 minutes (watching carefully) until the scalloped edge is toasted to a golden brown. Alternatively this works well with a cooks' blowtorch. This cake keeps beautifully stored in an airtight tin.

ALMOND ICING
Marzipan

Homemade almond icing is superior to the ready-made, so I've included it here if you have time to make it. A one-egg mix makes 375g, so you will probably have too much, in which case use the surplus to stuff dates or make some Stollen (see deliaonline.com).

90g icing sugar, plus extra for dusting ◆ 90g golden caster sugar
1 large egg, lightly beaten ◆ a few drops pure almond extract ◆ 1 teaspoon brandy
175g ground almonds ◆ a little icing sugar (to knead and roll)

Begin by sifting the icing sugar and caster sugar into a large bowl, then stir in the egg. Place the bowl over a pan of barely simmering water and whisk for about 10 minutes, until the mixture is thick and fluffy. Then remove the bowl from the heat and sit the base in about 5cm of cold water. Whisk in the almond extract and brandy and continue to whisk until the mixture is cool. At this point stir in the ground almonds and knead to form a firm paste on a surface lightly dusted with icing sugar.

Then roll out the amount needed on a clean surface dusted with icing sugar, and keep giving it quarter turns (to keep it round) between each roll. Once it is rolled to the right size, cover the top of the cake.

SUGARED FLOWERS

You won't believe how very easy this is, but there is a word of warning. Not all flowers are edible, so you need to do some research if you want to do something unusual. However, the good news is that unsprayed primroses and primulas are perfectly safe to eat (as are rose petals).

All you do is lightly beat an egg white with a teaspoon of water. Using a small soft brush lightly coat the surface of the petals, then sprinkle generously with caster sugar. Then leave them on a cake liner or some baking parchment to dry out completely (at least overnight). After that store them in an airtight container.

FONDANT ICING

This is for those who like a softer icing than royal icing, but prefer to have a homemade version.

250g fondant icing sugar ◆ *4–5 teaspoons water*

To roll: *1 tablespoon icing sugar* ◆ *1 dessertspoon cornflour*

Begin by sifting the icing sugar (all but 1 heaped tablespoon) into a large bowl and making a well in the centre. Add the water, a teaspoonful at a time, and stir with a wooden spoon until it is too stiff to stir any more. Then, using your hands, form the icing into a ball before turning out onto a clean, smooth, dry surface dusted with the reserved icing sugar, and knead for about 3 minutes until it becomes completely smooth (if the icing is sticky, knead in a little more icing sugar, or if it is dry run a little cold water over your fingers).

Then roll out the icing onto a clean surface dusted with a mixture of icing sugar and cornflour, and keep giving it quarter turns after each roll. Once it is rolled to the right size, ice the cake as soon as possible. If you want to make it ahead, it can be kept tightly wrapped in the fridge for 3 days (though once it is on the cake it does not need to be refrigerated).

SILVER ANGEL ICING

TOPS A 20CM ROUND CAKE

1 heaped tablespoon apricot jam ◆ *1 tablespoon brandy or Armagnac*
200g ready-made marzipan (or homemade, see page 200) ◆ *icing sugar, to dust*
250g white fondant icing (see page 203) ◆ *a little beaten egg white*
silver balls, to decorate

You will need a 10cm angel cookie cutter (see page 16)

First melt the jam with the brandy or Armagnac in a small saucepan, stirring until
all the lumps have dissolved. Now, using a brush, coat the top of the cake quite generously with
it. Then take the marzipan and roll it out on a surface lightly dusted with icing sugar and
cut out a 20cm circle. Then place this over the top of the cake.

Repeat with the icing and place this over the marzipan. Next, re-roll the trimmings and,
using the cutter, cut out an angel, dampen one side of it with cold water and then place this side
on top of the cake. After that, decorate the edges of the cake and the angel with silver balls, using
a little beaten egg white mixed with a little icing sugar as a glue to keep them in place. It's also
helpful to make some little indentations with the tip of a skewer first.

GOLDEN APRICOT & PECAN TOPPING

TOPS A 20CM ROUND CAKE

½g Radiant Gold edible lustre (see page 224)
approximately 26 pecan nuts, toasted (see page 42)
approximately 26 ready-to-eat dried apricots
2 tablespoons sieved apricot jam (or apricot glaze)
2 tablespoons brandy or Armagnac

You will need a small soft paintbrush (see page 224)

First use the dry paintbrush to gild half the toasted nuts and half the apricots. To do this dip the brush into the lustre and brush it all over one side of the fruits and the nuts. Use firm strokes of the brush and go over again and again until all of the top surface is bright shiny gold.

Then melt the jam with the brandy or Armagnac in a small saucepan, stirring until all the lumps have dissolved. Now, using a pastry brush, coat the top of the cake quite generously with it.

Next arrange a single row of the nuts and apricots down the centre of the cake. You can do any pattern you like but we have followed an order of pecan, gold pecan, apricot and gold apricot, then repeated this again and again (see photograph on page 196). Then we have simply repeated the rows either side of the central row but this time moved the position down slightly so the rows are irregular. When you get to the sides of the cake use a pair of scissors to trim the apricots so that they follow the line of the cake's edge.

Finally brush all of the non-gilded apricots and nuts with apricot glaze. You can safely do all this well ahead of time – it stays looking good for up to a month.

Dessert Cakes

VENETIAN ZABAGLIONE CAKE

SERVES 8

This is my adaptation of a cake still served in the famous Harry's Bar in Venice.
You can eat it sipping a Bellini cocktail or with coffee at any time of day. But for me,
lunch in the restaurant with this as a dessert has always been a sublime treat.

115g self-raising flour ◆ ½ level teaspoon baking powder ◆ 2 large eggs
115g spreadable butter ◆ 115g golden caster sugar ◆ ½ level teaspoon vanilla extract
a little icing sugar

For the filling: 3 large egg yolks ◆ 75g golden caster sugar ◆ 40g plain flour, sifted
250ml Marsala ◆ 340ml double cream

A 20cm round sponge tin (4cm deep), greased and base lined (see page 13),
plus two wire cooling trays

Begin by making the zabaglione filling. For this you need to take a medium-sized
bowl and in it beat the egg yolks for 1 minute with an electric hand whisk, then add the sugar
and whisk again until the mixture turns thick and pale – about 3 minutes. After that, add
a tablespoon of flour at a time and continue whisking till everything is smooth and
creamy, then gradually whisk in the Marsala.

Next transfer the mixture to a medium-sized saucepan and place it over a medium
heat, then take a wooden spoon and keep stirring the mixture until it has thickened and is just
about to come to simmering point. This usually takes about 5 minutes. Don't worry if it overheats
and begins to separate, just remove it from the heat and keep whisking until it is smooth again.
Transfer the mixture to a bowl, cover the surface of the mixture with clingfilm to stop a skin
forming and leave it to get completely cold. Then pop it in the fridge till needed.

To make the cake, begin by pre-heating the oven to 170°C, gas mark 3. Then sift the
flour and baking powder into a large roomy bowl, lifting the sieve high to give the flour an airing.
Now just add all the other ingredients (apart from the icing sugar) and, using the electric
hand whisk, whisk for about one minute until you have a smooth creamy mixture
that drops off a spoon easily.

Next, transfer the mixture into the tin, levelling it with the back of a spoon, and bake
near the centre of the oven for 30–35 minutes or until the centre feels springy. Leave the cake
in the tin for 5 minutes before loosening the edge by sliding a palette knife all round and
turning it out onto a cooling rack. Now peel off the base, place
another rack on top and flip it back over, then let it get quite cold.

To serve the cake, first whisk the zabaglione mixture to loosen it, then in a large bowl whisk
the cream till stiff and fold in the zabaglione. Next you need to place the cake on a flat surface
and, using a serrated palette knife, carefully slice it horizontally into two thin halves. Keep aside

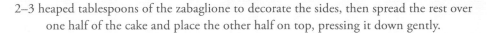

2–3 heaped tablespoons of the zabaglione to decorate the sides, then spread the rest over one half of the cake and place the other half on top, pressing it down gently.

Now carefully transfer the cake to a serving plate. Brush away any loose crumbs then, using a small palette knife, spread the rest of the filling all around the sides of the cake, and use the palette knife to make a vertical pattern, sliding the knife upwards from the base. Finally, dust the top of the cake with icing sugar. If you want to make this ahead of time, cover the cake with an upturned bowl and keep in the fridge (but remove it 30 minutes before serving).

CHOCOLATE SOUFFLÉ CAKE
with ARMAGNAC PRUNES & CRÈME FRAICHE SAUCE

SERVES 8

This is quite simply my own favourite chocolate dessert of all time. It's dark, very moist, and the prunes soaked in Armagnac make it a very grown-up chocolate experience. I used to call it Sunken Chocolate Cake but sometimes it doesn't sink! Either way it's glorious.

For the soufflé: 200g dark chocolate (minimum 70% cocoa solids) ◆ 110g unsalted butter 1 tablespoon Armagnac ◆ 4 large eggs, separated ◆ 110g golden caster sugar a little sifted icing sugar (or cocoa powder) for dusting

For the Armagnac prunes: 350g Agen no-soak prunes ◆ 150ml Armagnac

For the prune and crème fraiche sauce: the remainder of the soaked prunes 150ml crème fraiche

A 20cm loose-based round cake tin, greased and base lined (see page 13)

You need to begin this the night before. Although the prunes are no-soak we are still going to soak them so they can absorb all the wonderful flavour of Armagnac. Place them in a saucepan with 150ml of water and just bring it up to a gentle simmer. Then remove from the heat, pour everything into a bowl, add the Armagnac, leave it to cool, then cover and chill overnight.

When you are ready to make the cake, pre-heat the oven to 170°C, gas mark 3. Then break the chocolate into squares in a bowl, add the butter and sit the bowl over a saucepan containing about 5cm of barely simmering water (be careful that the bowl doesn't touch the water). This should take about 10 minutes to become melted, smooth and glossy. Then take the bowl off the heat, stir in the Armagnac and leave it to get cool.

Now you are going to need a large roomy bowl. In it whisk the egg yolks and caster sugar using an electric hand whisk for about 5 or 6 minutes, so that when you lift the whisk the mixture falls down making ribbon-like trails. Now take 18 of the pre-soaked prunes, halve them and stir the halves into the whisked egg mixture and follow that by adding the melted chocolate. Then give everything a good stir.

Now the whisk should be washed with hot soapy water and dried thoroughly to remove any traces of grease. The egg whites need to go into another large bowl and be whisked until they form soft peaks. After that, using a large metal spoon, fold them gently and carefully into the chocolate mixture.

Then, using the same spoon, transfer the mixture to the prepared tin and bake the cake on the centre shelf of the oven for about 30 minutes or until it's very puffy and the centre feels springy. When it's cooked allow it to cool in the tin and not to worry if it sinks a bit! When it's absolutely cold remove it from the tin (see page 12), peel off the lining, then cover with clingfilm, place in the fridge and allow it to chill for several hours.

Finally, make the sauce. Simply liquidise the prunes reserved from above together with their liquid. Place the purée in a serving bowl and lightly stir in the crème fraiche to give a slight marbled effect. When you are ready to serve the cake, dust the surface with icing sugar or cocoa (or a bit of each) and serve cut in slices with the sauce handed round separately.

Note: if you want to make this in advance the cake and the sauce can be frozen.

APRICOT HAZELNUT
MERINGUE CAKE
SERVES 6–8

This used to be a rather soft, rather squashy meringue, but now I like it crisper and chewier. Either way it's loved by everyone. You can of course use any other fruit – summer berries or in the winter passion fruit.

3 large egg whites ◆ 175g golden caster sugar
75g blanched hazelnuts, toasted (see page 42) and ground finely in a mini-chopper
275ml double cream ◆ whole toasted hazelnuts (to decorate)

For the filling: 150g ready-to-eat dried apricots, chopped
juice of 1 large orange and a 5cm strip of zest ◆ 4 tablespoons water
1 cinnamon stick, divided in half ◆ ½ teaspoon vanilla extract

Two 18cm by 4cm sponge tins, lightly buttered and bases lined (see page 13)
Pre-heat the oven to 150°C, gas mark 2

In a large bowl whisk the egg whites to the stiff peak stage. Then whisk in the sugar – roughly a tablespoon at a time. Next take a metal spoon and lightly and gently fold in the ground hazelnuts. Now divide the mixture between the prepared tins and spread it out as evenly as possible. Place the meringues near the centre of the oven and reduce the temperature to 140°C, gas mark 1. Allow them to cook for 1 hour, then turn the heat off and let the meringues cool in the oven. When they've cooled, loosen them round the edges with a palette knife. Place the base of each tin on an upturned bowl and just slide the tin downwards. After that use the palette knife to slide them onto a flat surface.

While the meringues are cooking, prepare the filling. Place all the ingredients (reserving half the orange juice for later) in a shallow pan, bring them up to simmering point then simmer gently for 30 minutes without a lid. After that, remove it from the heat, and when it's cooled remove the cinnamon sticks and the orange zest. Whizz half the mixture to a purée with the reserved orange juice in a mini-chopper. Then combine the purée with the rest.

To fill the meringues (which can be done up to 2 hours before serving), whip the cream to the soft peak stage, then carefully spread the cooled apricot mixture over one meringue, followed by half the whipped cream. Then, carefully, position the other meringue on top. Spread the remaining whipped cream over that and decorate round the edges with whole toasted hazelnuts. Use the base of the cake tin to transfer it to a serving plate. Then store covered in the fridge until needed.

Note: the meringues can be made several days ahead and stored in a tin, and freeze very well too.

PEAR & ALMOND CAKE
with STREUSEL TOPPING

SERVES 6–8

This would be my choice for autumn when there are lots of lovely ripe pears around. We like to eat it served in slices with pools of Jersey pouring cream.

For the cake: 110g self-raising flour ◆ 1 level teaspoon baking powder
50g spreadable butter ◆ 50g golden caster sugar ◆ 50g ground almonds ◆ 1 large egg
a few drops pure almond extract ◆ pinch of salt ◆ 3 tablespoons milk
2 ripe pears, peeled, cored and quartered, each quarter sliced into three

For the topping: 50g butter, melted ◆ 75g self-raising flour ◆ 50g demerara sugar
40g flaked almonds ◆ a dusting of icing sugar

A 20cm by 4cm sponge tin, lightly buttered and base lined (see page 13)
Pre-heat the oven to 200ºC, gas mark 6

All you do is sift the flour and baking powder into a roomy mixing bowl, lifting the sieve quite high to give the flour a good airing as it goes down, then simply add all the other ingredients (except the pears). Now, using an electric hand whisk, combine them for about 1 minute until you have a smooth creamy consistency. Next spoon the mixture into the prepared tin, and level off using the back of a tablespoon. Now arrange the pears in a circle on top (a few can go in the middle).

To make the topping, mix the flour and sugar in a bowl then add the melted butter and lightly crumble it with a fork. After that stir in the nuts, sprinkle the mixture all over the pears and bake near the centre of the oven for 45 minutes. Leave it to cool in the tin for 20 minutes before loosening the edge with a palette knife. Then place the tin on an upturned bowl and carefully slide the tin downwards (see page 12). After that use the palette knife to slide the cake off its liner onto a wire cooling rack. Just before serving, dust the surface with icing sugar.

HAZELNUT SHORTBREADS
with RASPBERRIES

SERVES 6

You can obviously use strawberries or indeed any summer berry mixture with these. They are extremely light, melt-in-the-mouth, and really taste of summer.

For the shortbreads: 85g blanched hazelnuts, toasted (see page 42) ◆ 110g block butter, softened 50g golden icing sugar ◆ 110g plain flour, sifted ◆ 50g rice flour or ground rice, sifted

For the raspberry purée: 175g raspberries ◆ 1½ level tablespoons golden caster sugar

For the confectioners' custard: 1 level tablespoon custard powder 1 level tablespoon golden caster sugar ◆ 100ml milk ◆ 3 large egg yolks 200ml crème fraiche ◆ 2 teaspoons vanilla extract ◆ 100ml double cream, whipped

To serve: 300g raspberries (reserve 18 to decorate) ◆ a dusting of icing sugar

Two large baking trays with non-stick liners, and a 9cm round pastry cutter Pre-heat the oven to 180°C, gas mark 4

Start off by grinding the hazelnuts finely using a mini-chopper or processor.

Now, in a mixing bowl, cream the butter and icing sugar together until light and fluffy, then gradually work in the sifted flours, followed by the ground hazelnuts, bringing the mixture together into a stiff ball. Place the dough in a polythene bag and leave in the fridge to rest for 1 hour. After that, roll it out to a thickness of 3–4mm, stamp out as many rounds as you can by placing the cutter on the pastry and giving it a sharp tap, then simply lift the cutter and the piece will drop out. Re-roll any trimmings to cut out more (to make a total of 12). Now arrange the biscuits on the baking trays and lightly prick each one with a fork. Bake one tray at a time near the centre of the oven for 10–12 minutes. Leave on the baking trays to cool for about 10 minutes, then carefully remove to a wire rack to cool completely.

While the shortbreads are cooling, purée the raspberries with the sugar in a mini-chopper or processor and pass through a nylon sieve to remove the seeds, then place in a bowl, cover and chill till needed.

For the custard filling: place the custard powder and sugar in a bowl and mix to a smooth paste with the milk and egg yolks. Then heat the crème fraiche in a saucepan and when it begins to bubble, pour it in to join the custard mixture. Whisk everything together, then return it to the saucepan and, still whisking, bring it up to a simmer. When it begins to boil it becomes thick, so remove it from the heat, add the vanilla extract, then pour it into a bowl to cool. When the custard is cold, fold it into the whipped cream. Cover and chill till needed.

Just before serving, spread equal quantities of the custard-cream mixture over 6 of the biscuits, then arrange the raspberries on top, not forgetting to reserve 18. Spoon equal quantities of the purée over, then sandwich by lightly placing the other shortbreads on top. Finally, sprinkle with a dusting of icing sugar and top with the remaining raspberries.

Note: while everything can be prepared well in advance, it's important not to assemble the shortbreads until just before serving.

LEMON GRIESTORTE

SERVES 6

Because there's no flour in this it's unimaginably light and airy, and very lemony,
which makes it a very elegant dessert cake.

3 large eggs, separated ◆ *110g golden caster sugar* ◆ *zest of 1 large lemon and ½ the juice*
50g semolina ◆ *1 tablespoon ground almonds*

For the filling and topping: 4 tablespoons lemon curd (see page 34)
150ml double cream, whipped ◆ *icing sugar*

Two 18cm by 4cm sponge tins, lightly buttered and bases lined (see page 13),
plus two wire cooling trays
Pre-heat the oven to 180°C, gas mark 4

After separating the eggs, place the yolks in a mixing bowl, then add the sugar and
lemon juice and whisk until the mixture is thick and beginning to turn paler. Now fold in the
lemon zest, semolina and ground almonds until everything is evenly blended.

After that, wash the whisk and dry it very thoroughly (so it's absolutely grease-free) and
whisk the egg whites in a roomy bowl up to the soft peak stage. Now take a metal spoon and
very carefully and gently fold them into the egg yolk mixture.

Next divide the mixture between the two prepared tins, level off using the back of a tablespoon
and bake near the centre of the oven for about 20–25 minutes. They are cooked when you press
lightly with your little finger and the centre springs back. Let the cakes cool in the tins for 10
minutes before loosening the edges by sliding a palette knife all round and turning them out onto
a cooling tray. Now carefully peel back the lining by gently pulling it back. Lightly place the other
cooling tray on top and just flip them both over so that the tops are facing upwards (this is to
prevent them sticking to the cooling tray).

When they are absolutely cold, place one cake on a serving dish and spread with lemon curd and
whipped cream, then place the other cake on top and dust generously with sieved icing sugar.
Store in a polythene box in the fridge.

SPICED APPLE & CIDER CAKE

SERVES 8

This is quite definitely a dessert cake. The combination of spices, the hint of orange
and the balance of tart apples and cake are perfect. It needs a large dollop of crème fraiche
or whipped cream to go with it.

1 smallish Bramley apple ◆ 150ml dry cider ◆ 75g raisins ◆ 225g self-raising flour
1 level teaspoon baking powder ◆ 1 level teaspoon ground cinnamon
½ level teaspoon ground cloves ◆ ¼ whole nutmeg, freshly grated
150g spreadable butter ◆ 2 large eggs, beaten ◆ 150g light brown soft sugar

For the topping: 25g spreadable butter ◆ 25g self-raising flour
50g light brown soft sugar ◆ 1 level teaspoon ground cinnamon
¼ level teaspoon ground cloves ◆ 25g flaked almonds
2 smallish Bramley apples ◆ a dusting of golden icing sugar

A 20cm loose-based round cake tin, greased and base lined (see page 13)
Pre-heat the oven to 180°C, gas mark 4

First chop the apple (no need to peel) and put it into a bowl with the cider and raisins
while you prepare the cake.

Sift the flour, baking powder and spices into a roomy mixing bowl, lifting the sieve
quite high to give the flour a good airing as it goes down. Then add the butter, eggs and sugar.
Now, using an electric hand whisk, combine them for about one minute until you have a smooth
creamy consistency. Then, using a large metal spoon, fold in the apple, raisins and cider. Spoon
the mixture into the prepared tin, and level the top with the back of the spoon.

Now for the topping: measure the butter, flour, sugar, cinnamon and cloves into a bowl.
Rub the mixture with your fingertips until you have a fairly coarse, crumbly mixture, then add
the flaked almonds. Now, quickly quarter, core and peel the remaining two apples. Slice them
thinly and scatter the slices all over the top of the cake. Then sprinkle the topping over the apples
and bake the cake near the centre of the oven for 1 hour 20 minutes to 1 hour 40 minutes or
until the cake shows signs of shrinking away from the side of the tin.

Leave it to cool in the tin for 10 minutes, then loosen it round the edge with a palette knife.
Place the tin on an upturned bowl and slide the tin downwards (see page 12). Then, using the
palette knife, carefully slide it onto a cooling rack to finish cooling. Dust with a little golden
icing sugar before serving. Store in an airtight tin.

BAKED VANILLA CHEESECAKE
with CARAMEL SAUCE

SERVES 8

I have made many cheesecakes over the years but this one is my current favourite. Part of its charm is that it's a little bit wobbly at the end of the cooking time and goes on firming up as it cools and chills. This makes it extra specially soft and luscious.

For the base: 200g shortbread fingers ◆ 50g block butter, melted

For the filling: 300g full fat cream cheese ◆ 175g golden caster sugar
25g plain flour ◆ 350ml crème fraiche ◆ 3 large eggs, beaten
1 dessertspoon vanilla extract

For the caramel sauce: 250g white granulated sugar ◆ 3 tablespoons hot water
150ml double cream ◆ 1 teaspoon vanilla extract

A 20cm by 4cm round sponge tin, greased and lined (see page 13), plus a medium heavy-based saucepan
Pre-heat the oven to 150°C, gas mark 2

First blitz the biscuits into crumbs in a food processor, then tip them into a bowl, add the melted butter and give it a thorough mix. Next press the crumbs evenly into the base of the lined tin using the back of a metal spoon to give it a smooth surface.

Now make the filling. In a bowl, mix together the cream cheese, caster sugar and flour. Then stir in the crème fraiche, beaten eggs and vanilla.

Pour half the mixture over the biscuit base and place it on the lowest shelf of the oven, then pour in the other half. Bake for 55 minutes, by which time the cheesecake will be barely coloured; it should be just set firm on the edge but still slightly wobbly in the centre. Now turn the oven off and leave the cheesecake in the oven to cool completely, before placing in the fridge for several hours to firm up. Once chilled, the cheesecake can be removed from its tin (see page 12) and placed on a serving dish.

To make the caramel sauce: put the granulated sugar into the saucepan over a very gentle heat. While the sugar is heating (which will take about 7 minutes) shake the pan every now and then to move it around and prevent it caramelising in patches before all the sugar has had time to dissolve.

When all the sugar has melted, turn the heat up to high so the liquid begins to bubble and darken. Stir and simmer until the mixture becomes the colour of dark honey (but watch it carefully as it only takes a few seconds to turn from caramel to burnt sugar!). Take the pan off the heat and add the hot water – this will make it splutter but this will soon die down. Now add the cream and vanilla, and stir to combine well. Leave to cool, and store in a lidded container. Serve in a jug to pour over the cheesecake at the table.

SPECIALIST SUPPLIERS

For information about stockists of the Deliaonline Silverwood bakeware and Deliaonline Bake-O-Glide tin liners go to www.deliaonline.com

Arthur Price
www.arthurprice.com

Britannia Way
Lichfield
Staffordshire
WS14 9UY

enquiries@arthurprice.com
Tel: 01543 257 775

Old English Fiddle spoons (stainless steel).

Cake Craft Kiosk
www.cakecraftkiosk.co.uk

The Old Corn Dryer
Girls School Lane
Butterwick
Boston
PE22 0HZ

Tel: 08432 891 766

Football Flags.

Cakes Cookies & Crafts Shop
www.cakescookiesandcraftsshop.co.uk

Unit 2, Francis Business Park
White Lund Industrial Estate
Morecambe
Lancashire
LA3 3PT

Tel: 01524 389 684

Cellophane bags, cake boards, coloured cupcake and muffin cases, standard baking cases, silver foil muffin cases. Radiant gold lustre, food colouring pastes and powders, gingerbread man cutter and sugarcraft brushes.

Country Products
www.countryproducts.co.uk

Unit 6 Centre Park
Tockwith
North Yorkshire
YO26 7QF

Tel: 01423 358 858

For glacé pineapple, angelica, golden glacé cherries, green glacé cherries, whole pieces of candied citron, orange peel and lemon peel. They also do maple syrup Amber no.2, Fairtrade golden syrup, vanilla extract, almond extract, fine and medium ground oatmeal, semolina, ground rice, coconut milk powder, dried fruits, blanched peanuts and blanched hazelnuts.

David Mellor Design
www.davidmellordesign.com

4 Sloane Square
London
SW1W 8EE

Tel: 020 7730 4259

Kitchenware.

Divertimenti

www.divertimenti.co.uk

227-229 Brompton Road
London
SW3 2EP

Tel: 0870 129 5026

Kitchenware.

The Fairtrade Foundation

www.fairtrade.org.uk

The Fairtrade Foundation
3rd Floor
Ibex House
42-47 Minories
London EC3N 1DY

Tel: 020 7405 5942

For information about Fairtrade
products and stockists.

Fine Cut Sugarcraft Shop

www.finecutsugarcraft.com

Workshop 4, Old Stable Block
Holme Pierrepont Hall
Holme Pierrepont
Nottingham
NG12 2LD

Tel: 0115 933 4349

Angel cutter for Christmas cake
decoration.

Lakeland

www.lakeland.co.uk

Alexandra Buildings
Windermere
Cumbria
LA23 1BQ

Tel: 01539 488 100

2lb traditional loaf liners, parchment
cake-tin base liners, mini parchment
roll for the sides of tins, 18cm liners
for Parkin, parchment-lined foil;
general kitchenware.

Meadowsweet Flowers

www.meadowsweetflowers.co.uk

Limeslake Farm
South Molton
Devon
EX36 3LY

info@meadowsweetflowers.co.uk

Crystallised edible flowers.

Seasoned Pioneers

www.seasonedpioneers.co.uk

Unit 8 Stadium Court
Stadium Road
Plantation Business Park
Bromborough
Wirral
CH62 3RP

Tel: 0800 068 2348

Spices in foil pouches.

Tesco

www.tesco.com

Tel: 08457 225 533

Plastic 4-litre mixing bowls.

INDEX

ACKNOWLEDGEMENTS

My profound thanks to Lindsey Greensted Benech, who should in truth be acknowledged as the co-author of this book. We have worked side by side from the beginning, proving always that two heads are better than one. 'What do you think, Lindsey?' has been my mantra throughout.

Thanks to the rest of the team: Melanie, Jane and Julia. Also to Caroline Liddell and John Tovey, whose recipes and help contributed greatly to the success of the first edition in 1977. Finally, a huge thank you to Elizabeth Hallett without whom this book would never have existed.

Photography *Dan Jones*
Photographer's Assistant *Andrew Burton*
Designer *Paul Webster*
Props Styling *Penny Markham*
Copy editor *Bryony Nowell*
Proofreaders *Annie Lee and Miren Lopategui*
Indexer *Caroline Wilding*

First published as
Delia Smith's Book of Cakes
in Great Britain in 1977 by Coronet Books
Reprinted 25 times
This revised and updated edition first
published in Great Britain in 2013
by Hodder & Stoughton
An Hachette UK company

1

A CIP catalogue record for this title is available from the British Library

Hardback
ISBN 978 1 444 73481 2
eBook
ISBN 978 1 444 73484 3

Printed and bound in Germany by Mohn Media

Hodder & Stoughton policy is to use papers that are natural, renewable
and recyclable products and made from wood grown in sustainable forests.
The logging and manufacturing processes are expected to conform to the
environmental regulations of the country of origin

Hodder & Stoughton Ltd
338 Euston Road
London NW1 3BH

www.hodder.co.uk